THE TEMPLE

JOHN M. LUNDQUIST

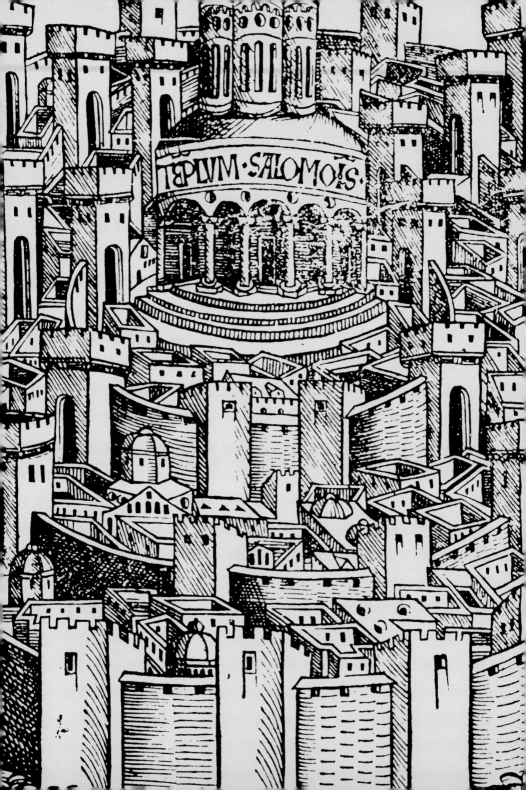

TEPLVM·SALOMOIS·

ART+IMAGINATION

JOHN M. LUNDQUIST

THE TEMPLE

Meeting Place of Heaven and Earth

137 illustrations, 42 in colour

Thames & Hudson

To my children

Page 2 | The Dome of the Rock from Hartmann Schedel's *Nuremberg Chronicle*, 1493.
Pages 4–5 | Maya sarcophagus lid depicting the soul's journey after death.

ART+IMAGINATION

GENERAL EDITOR: Jill Purce

First published in the United Kingdom in 1993 by
THAMES & HUDSON LTD, 181A High Holborn, London WC1V 7QX

This edition 2012

Copyright © 1993 and 2012 THAMES & HUDSON LTD, London

DESIGNED by BARNBROOK

British Library Cataloguing-in-Publication Data
A catalogue record for this book is available from the British Library

ISBN 978-0-500-81050-7

Printed and bound in China by Toppan Leefung

To find out about all our publications, please visit *www.thamesandhudson.com*
There you can subscribe to our e-newsletter, browse or download
our current catalogue, and buy any titles that are in print.

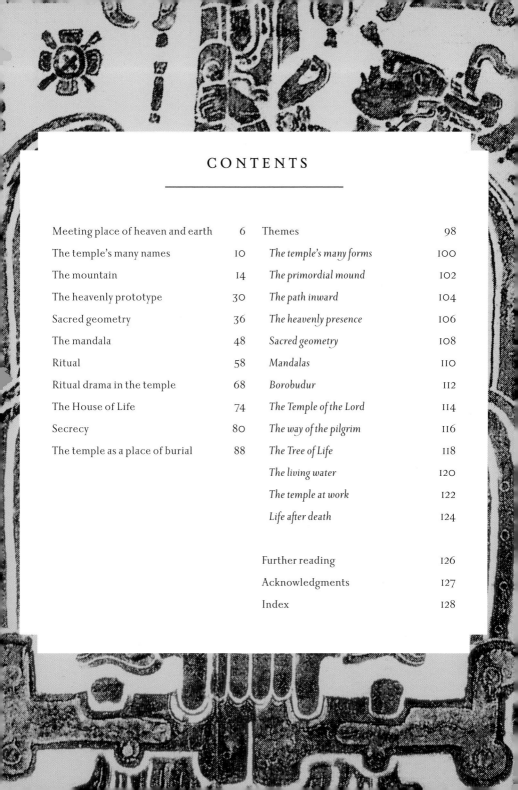

CONTENTS

THE temple incorporates within itself most of the ideas that make up our concept of religion. These include the idea of the centre, the sacred mountain, sacred waters and trees of life, sacred geometry, orientation to the four cardinal directions, initiation ritual, sacred dance, the mysteries, New Year festivals, ideas of cosmos/chaos and creation myths. It was within the setting of the temple that these other symbols, rituals and sacred textual traditions arose, and it is within the temple that they still have their deepest and truest meaning. Indeed, they can only be fully understood when they are reincorporated back into the context of the temple, and seen in that wider relationship.

➤ The idea of the temple as the house of God, a place in which the spirit resides, is common to all religions. In this late 15th-century altar by Crivelli, the Madonna della Rondine, St Jerome (right) holds a model of the Temple of Jerusalem from which the golden rays of divinity are radiating.

Throughout all time, the temple has been the repository of the esoteric tradition. It was in the temple, and in the temple alone, that the knowledge of the mysteries could be found. These mysteries were recorded in books kept in the temple libraries, called 'Houses of Life' in ancient Egypt. But it was not a matter of 'book learning' alone, since the knowledge and understanding of the mysteries could only be transmitted through initiation ritual.

A pre-Aztec model of a temple, from the Aztec river region of Mexico.

ICY EST LE HAVLT
ROCH QVI LES
NVES SVRPASSE
DES PLVS HAVLX
DV MODE . . . AV

We can now begin to see how much more fundamental the temple is as the central ritual structure of the religious life than is commonly understood. If, in any religious culture, the temple dies out, as it did in Judaism for example after the destruction of the Temple of Jerusalem in AD 70, at least two things happen: firstly, the scriptural and ritual tradition, which takes its meaning from the context of the temple, becomes, in the phrase of Jacob Neusner, a 'map without territory'. The ritual laws, the initiation rituals, become suspended in space, as it were, without a place in which they can be practised; and secondly, much of the ritual-initiation practice, previously carried out in an elaborate architectural setting, is transformed into a mental process; everything goes inward, is transferred onto the human body, and the mystical tradition is born.

Throughout all time, the temple has been the repository of the esoteric tradition. It was in the temple, and in the temple alone, that the knowledge of the mysteries could be found.

This mystical tradition is, by definition, the transferral of the esoteric rituals and instructions from the sacred temple building into the mind of the practitioner. In Neusner's terms the 'territory' of the 'map' becomes the psychic processes of the individual. However, the body can also be at the ritual centre of temple initiation, as is the case in Indian Shiva temple ritual. The primordial creator god of Hinduism, Prajapati, became Purusa, the cosmic, universal person, whose sacrificed body was incorporated into the mandala floor plan of the Hindu temple.

◄— In this 16th-century painting of the 'Montagne de la Sagesse' by Jean Lemaire de Belges, wisdom is represented as a city on a steep hill, to which hard study is the arduous and only path for the individual.

THE TEMPLE'S MANY NAMES

'TEMPLUM', says the 1st-century BC Roman writer Varro, 'is the name given to a place set aside and limited by certain formulaic words for the purpose of augury or the taking of auspices.' From this come our words 'temple' and 'contemplate', which refer to the sacred, demarcated zone of the temple, that which was within the augur's range of vision, that which he 'contemplated'. Where there is no temple, there is, strictly speaking, no 'contemplation'.

There are three world regions in the cosmos: the sky, the earth and the underworld, all of which are united in the temple.

The Latin root *tem* (to cut) has a cognate in Greek, *temno*, from which the word *temenos* derives. A *temenos* was 'a precinct, a piece of land marked off from common uses and dedicated to a god'. We now use *temenos* to mean the platform on which the temple building stands – an architectural structure that separated the building off from common, everyday activities. But the Greek root has a much more ancient predecessor in Sumerian, *temen*, which meant a heaped-up pile of earth, as in the name of the Neo-Babylonian ziggurat (the traditional Tower of Babel), the *E-Temen-An-Ki*, the 'House of the Foundation of Heaven and Earth'.

➝ According to the Bible, a tower was constructed in Babylon to connect the earthly world to the heavens. In this 1563 representation of the Tower of Babel by Pieter Bruegel the Elder (detail) the structure resembles a ziggurat, or stepped pyramid, such as the *E-Temen-An-Ki* in Babylon.

Varro, in *De Lingua Latina*, states that there are three temples: of the sky, of the earth and of the underworld. We see this reflected in the Babylonian temple name and it brings us to the universal idea that there are three world regions in the cosmos: the sky, the earth and the underworld, all of which are united in the temple, with its central pillar (sometimes, as in Scandinavia, a world-tree), connecting the three zones.

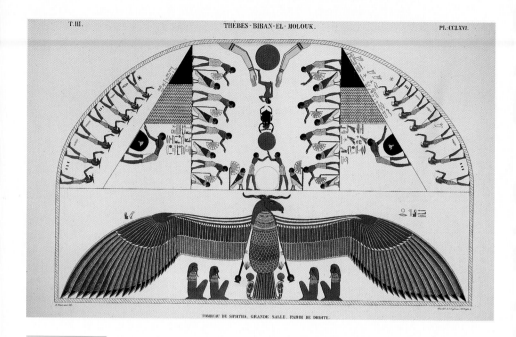

TOMBEAU DE SIPHTHA. GRANDE SALLE. PAROI DE DROITE.

The Egyptian book of caverns from the tomb of Tausert, Thebes, shows the sun as centre of the universe. It is represented in three ways – as a child (inverted, moved by a pair of arms), as a ram-headed beetle and as a red disc – surrounded by worshippers.

We see this concept in ancient Sumer in one of the names given to a temple by King Gudea of Lagash, *temen abzu*, the Foundation of the Abyss. The *temen* in ancient Sumerian cosmology was seen as sunk down into the abyss. The temple pillars extended into the underworld regions, tying this region of the cosmos together with the earth and the sky.

The most common name for ancient Egyptian temples, *hwt ntr*, signified the manor or mansion of the god, the place where he lived, and where his ritual worship took place. Texts inscribed on the inner sanctum walls of the Ptolemaic Period Temple of Edfu called that temple 'Foundation Ground of the Gods of the Beginnings', while the inner sanctum itself was called 'The High Seat', that is, the mythical mound of primordial creation (*p. 86*).

The most widely known name for Hindu temples, Prasada, 'is made up of the presence of Shiva and Shakti, and of the Principles and Forms of Existence from the elementary substance Earth and ending with Shakti. The concrete form of Shiva is called House of God. So one should contemplate and worship it first' (Kramrisch). The Prasada is brought into existence by the mantra *Nadi*, the primary vibration in the universe. In ancient Egypt, at Edfu, the temple was seen as coming into existence by the very process of the naming of its parts.

Deep within the temple, in its womb, reside the sacred relics, with their *dhatus* (magic elements).

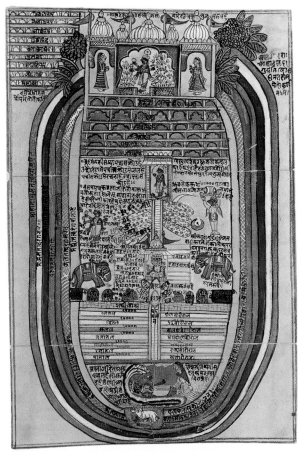

In Buddhism, one of the commonest names for the temple is 'pagoda'. This word comes from the Sanskrit *dhatu-gharba* in which *dhatu* refers to the magical, sacred relics, particularly those related to the Buddha himself, which were kept in the temple, and *gharba* refers to the 'womb', the innermost sanctuary of the temple, which in Hindu temples were built deep within the centre of the structure, like a dark cave within a mountain. From *dhatu-gharba* comes the Sinhalese *dagoba*, which in Burma and other Southeast Asian countries becomes 'pagoda'. The corresponding Sanskrit term is *stupa*, from Sanskrit *stup*, 'to accumulate or gather together'. Thus, deep within the temple, in its womb (in Buddhist pagodas or stupas the *harmika* or relic chamber is located above the domical base, which represents the *anda* or 'world-egg'), reside the sacred relics, with their *dhatus* (magic elements), which, like the egg, possess the power of life. The power of this womb and its world-egg is transferred through the sacred altar that stands over the *gharba*, namely the *harmika*, and becomes a force for spiritual life and renewal.

The universe hatched from a cosmic egg, shown in an 18th-century painting from Rajasthan. The god Vishnu is at the bottom of the womb-egg, above him are the seven levels of the underworld, and above them is the earth. At the top, Krishna dwells in paradise.

IN the beginning, there was water. Water has a two-fold imagery, life-giving and destructive. These two aspects, each represented by its avatar, fought one another at the beginning of the creative process, as described, for example, in the Babylonian creation account, *Enuma Elish*. The battle was won by the forces of cosmos (in the case of *Enuma Elish* this was Marduk), which defeated the chaotic waters and their serpent deity (in *Enuma Elish*, Tiamat). With the end of this conflict, the waters subsided, and there appeared a mound of earth, the primary and primordial ground of creation, where the deity first appeared. This mound, charged with the energy of primordial life, became transformed into the sacred mountain, the most holy place on earth, the archetype of the temple. In virtually all cultures, temples are either the architectural representation of the primordial mound or of a world mountain or some combination of these two.

In virtually all cultures, temples are either the architectural representation of the primordial mound or of a world mountain or some combination of these two.

The Step Pyramid introduced by the Egyptian king Zoser in the Third Dynasty was an architectural realization of the primordial hill, which was then modified into the true pyramid in the Fourth Dynasty. During the Ptolemaic Period, every temple was considered to be a replica of the primeval temple, which had been built upon the primordial mound after it had emerged from Nun, the primeval waters.

The canonical foundation ceremonies for temples in ancient Egypt included one ritual, 'hoeing the earth', that is directly related to the concept that the temple is the upward architectural extension out of the primeval waters of creation leading up into the sky above the primordial mound. In this ritual, the king would dig a pit with a hoe down to the water line. This founded the temple in the primordial waters.

→ The pyramids of Giza, man-made mountains, are the most perfectly geometrical of sacred structures.

The same conceptions are found in ancient Judaism, with the difference that in the place of the primeval mound a Foundation Stone appears. A famous passage in the Midrash Tanhuma states:

> Just as the navel is found at the centre of a human being, so the land of Israel is found at the centre of the world. Jerusalem is at the centre of the land of Israel, and the temple is at the centre of Jerusalem, the Holy of Holies is at the centre of the temple, the Ark is at the centre of the Holy of Holies, and the Foundation Stone is in front of the Ark, which spot is the foundation of the world.

In ancient Israel, this Foundation Stone played the same role as the primordial mound in Egypt: it was the first solid material to emerge from the waters of creation, and it was upon this stone that the deity effected creation. According to Jewish legend, it was this primordial rock on which Jacob slept, at the place he subsequently named Bethel (Genesis 28). This same rock then came to be placed in the Holy of Holies of the Temple of Solomon, and, according to Islamic tradition, it is this same rock from which the Prophet Mohammed ascended into heaven, over which the second most sacred mosque of Islam, the Dome of the Rock, is built.

In ancient Sumer, the innermost sanctuary was sometimes referred to as the 'holy mound', and was seen as the mound which arose out of the primordial abyss. In this room the most sacred functions of Sumero-Babylonian religion were carried out. The temple itself grew up out of the abyss, in which it was founded, and became like a great mountain. The Holy of Holies of the main temple to the god Assur in ancient Assyria was called 'house of the great mountain of the lands'.

◄— The remains of the Babylonian ziggurat at Aqar Quf, a man-made structure that has weathered so the exterior appears like a naturally formed rock.

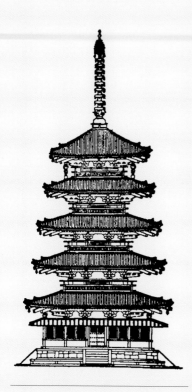

The Buddhist Horyuji pagoda in Japan is the centrepiece of the country's oldest temple complex. Built around a central pillar, it enshrines symbolic relics of the Buddha.

→ Rising through many storeys the Porcelain Tower of Nanjing in China, drawn here by a European artist in the 17th century, was yet another stylized version of a mountain.

Perhaps no culture has so thoroughly created the architectural equivalent of a mountain in its temples as the Khmers of Cambodia, who, in the temples at Angkor, reproduced the mythical five peaks of the world mountain of the Hindu tradition, Mount Meru. And since Mount Meru, as the axis of the universe, was seen as reaching deep into the underworld, the bases of the Baphuon temple at Angkor were constructed in such a manner that they could not be seen. An inscription that relates to the Mebon Oriental pyramidal temple at Angkor states: 'In the middle of the sea, which is the sacred pool of Yasodhara, he erected a mountain, with a summit like that of Meru, covered with temples and sanctuaries plastered in stucco.'

Ancient Indian texts list the first three types of temple as Meru, Mandara and Kailasa, all of which are names given in the Indian tradition to the world mountain, which forms the axis of the universe.

The temple is a visual representation of all the symbolism of the mountain, and thus the architecture reflects this symbolism in a thoroughgoing and repetitive way (for example, the pagoda structures of Indian, Chinese, Southeast Asian and Japanese temple architecture, with the multi-level hipped roofs present on every building and gateway in the complex, or the Prasada of the Hindu temple), and is a constant visual reminder that the visitor/initiate is engaged on a journey up a mountain, to heaven.

A lavish Indian ceremony, including a horse and an elephant, passing the temple of Srirangam, India, dating from around 1800.

The mountain, a powerful earthly centre and point of contact with the heavens, became a gathering place for the celebration of seasonal rituals and for renewal ceremonies at the New Year. One of the main purposes of the New Year festivals was to rededicate the temple, to reestablish and reaffirm the peoples' connection with the gods in the heavens. Numerous temple reliefs, as well as reliefs on the walls of cities near the main gateways, depict the processions of kings and nobles, foreign peoples bearing fabulous gifts, all kinds of wheeled vehicles, and animals, approaching the city in order to attend the New Year festivals, where the rededication of the temple would signal the resumption of cosmic union and harmony.

The vegetation that the waters produced, which we can equate with the 'tree of life', was luxurious, pristine and life-giving. This symbolism is exceptionally vivid in the Old Testament in reference to the messianic temple of the end of time, for example in Ezekiel: 'Then he brought me back to the door of the temple; and behold, water was issuing from below the threshold of the temple toward the east ... (47:1) And on the banks, on both sides of the river, there will grow all kinds of trees for food' (47:12).

→ Water, which moves like a living being, has always been an image of the life of the spirit. Christ's own metaphor is represented in literal terms in this 9th-century Gospel book. The fountain is itself like a miniature temple.

Stone has played a part in worship for thousands of years. These stelae at Hazor, a Canaanite shrine near the Sea of Galilee, remain powerfully evocative of the worship of the moon-goddess.

Other sources indicate that these waters flowed out from under the Holy of Holies, and were in fact held or capped in place by the Rock of Foundation or Foundation Stone, the Hebrew version of the primordial mound. A Neo-Sumerian temple hymn celebrates the temple with the line, 'Temple, at its top a mountain, at its bottom a spring.' Another ancient temple was referred to in an inscription as 'the House of the Plant of Life'. Temple architecture, paintings and reliefs depicted the 'primordial landscape', the world as it was in the beginning – mound, waters and trees of life (or other kinds of vegetation) in or near the Holy of Holies. An ancient Indian text states that 'The gods always play where groves are near, by rivers, mountains and springs, and in towns with pleasure gardens.' When King Jayavarman VII restored Angkor in the late 12th century he had an inscription recorded at the four corners of the city which compared the wall of the city to the mountain chain that surrounds the universe, and the moat to the primeval ocean.

Byblos in Lebanon, a city on the sea, housed important stone temples in the ancient world. The tall obelisks, once capped with gold, stood in two rows around a rectangular enclosure.

Within the mystical Islamic traditions the heavenly throne was said to rest on the primordial waters, which represented the entirety of the creation – spiritual and material. The heavenly throne descended to the earth, forming the Kaabah in Mecca. Each of the four elements of the universe is represented in one of the four walls of the Kaabah (earth, air, fire, water), since the temple is the mirror image of the cosmos. Of these four, the north-east, or *Iraqi* corner, represents the primordial waters, and it is at this corner that the Zamzam well is located, out of which arise the living waters.

It is also at the north-east corner of the Kaabah that the Black Stone that embodies the essence and secret of the temple itself is to be found. According to Shiite Islamic tradition, the Black Stone originated as an angel who instructed Adam in the Garden of Eden. This angel had been the first in heaven to agree to covenant with God, and God had designated him as the one before whom all humankind would covenant each year. Upon Adam's expulsion from the Garden of Eden, this angel had taken the appearance of a White Pearl. Outside of the Garden, where Adam could no longer remember the promises he had made in the Garden, he noticed the White Pearl, but saw in it only a common stone. The Pearl then spoke to Adam, reminding him of the experiences in Eden. Adam then recognized his true self, kissed the Pearl, and renewed his covenant with God, promising that for ever after his posterity would likewise covenant themselves with God. The Pearl was then transformed into a Black Stone, symbolizing the darkness of this world, and it was this Stone that Adam, accompanied by the angel Gabriel, carried with him on his journey to Mecca. Upon his arrival in Mecca, the angels of heaven constructed a temple there that was the image of the temple where they had dwelt in heaven. Likewise, just as in heaven an angel had been the first to take an oath before God, so now that same angel, transformed into the Black Stone, was placed in the north-east corner of the Kaabah, so that the ritual of heaven could be performed yearly in the temple on earth. Thus, at the north-east corner of the Kaabah, pilgrims encounter both the Waters of Life, in the Zamzam well, and the Black Stone, which symbolizes the recovery of the Paradisical situation of the Garden of Eden, and the establishment on earth of the heavenly model.

Just as was the case with the Stone of Foundation that was presumed to have been located within the Holy of Holies of the Temple of Solomon, so also the Black Stone of the Kaabah was the umbilicus terrae, the navel of the earth, the primary centre of the earth, and the place of initial creation. Indeed, in the early centuries after Christ's death, Christians generally believed that the Temple Mount had been superseded by Christ's burial place as the most holy place in Christendom, just as the New Testament had superseded the Old in Christian theology.

The Black Stone of the Kaabah is placed at Mecca, as illustrated in a 17th-century manuscript, the *Rawdat al-Safa*, by Mirkhwand. The Black Stone is in the north-east corner of the Kaabah, next to a holy well – uniting water and stone.

One of the most interesting ancient expressions of the association of temple and primeval waters is found in the account of the Temple of Atargatis in the north Syrian town of Hierapolis by the Syro-Greek writer Lucian. He reports that the inhabitants of the city believed that their temple had been founded over a 'chasm', which, following the end of the Great Flood, had opened up in the city and had swallowed up the flood waters. It was Deucalion, the Greek Noah, who had then built altars and a temple on the site of the chasm. In order to memorialize this event, the inhabitants of the entire area of north Syria would go twice yearly in formal processions to the sea where they would fetch water that would be returned to the temple and poured into the crevice inside the temple.

The Germanic and Scandinavian peoples also viewed mountains as particularly sacred. Place names that have been preserved in northern Europe, such as Wodansberge (the mountain of Wotan), and Odinsberg (in Scandinavia, the mountain of Odin), bear testimony to this. As was widely the case in antiquity, the coronation of the king, the decree of new laws or law codes, and other important royal acts were carried out in Scandinavia on the sacred mountain (or in its architectural counterpart, the temple). The Icelandic sacred place was the *Lögberg*, or 'law rock', located on a natural or man-made high place, where laws were decreed and where the king performed his royal functions.

According to Scandinavian mythology a gigantic world-tree, Yggdrassil, united the three main world regions, with its roots sinking deep into the earth, while its branches reached into the heavens. A serpent lay at its roots; and an eagle nested in its heights. A number of sacred springs arose out of the depths of the earth at the tree's roots, including the spring of Mimir, the spring of wisdom and of life's mysteries. The springs at the roots of Yggdrassil restored one to health, as did the moisture that constantly dropped from its branches. The medieval historian Adam of Bremen, to whom we are indebted for a partial picture of the great Norse temple at Uppsala, in Sweden, reports that there was a huge evergreen flourishing at the temple. A spring emerged at its roots, to which sacrifices were made.

According to Scandinavian mythology a gigantic world-tree, Yggdrassil, united the three main world regions, with its roots sinking deep into the earth, while its branches reached into the heavens.

The Scandinavian world-tree is at the centre of the mythology of the Scandinavian shaman deity, Odin. A well-known phrase in the poem *Hávámal* depicts Odin hanging on the tree, pierced with a spear: 'Nine nights I hung on the tree, wounded by a spear, dedicated to Odin, I myself to myself. I hung on a tree of which no one knows from which roots it grows ... I sought below and lifted up the runic letters and I fell down from the tree' (trans. Hollander). The roots of the tree are in the underworld, the world of the dead, from which the spring Mimir, wisdom and divine knowledge, emerges. The shaman uses the world-tree as a vehicle to traverse the three cosmic zones, the heaven, the earth and the underworld, since it encompasses all of these.

◄ Even today the tree is used as a sacred space; a wayside shrine in Italy is placed within a circular cage of pollarded branches.

The cross on which Jesus was crucified carried similar symbolism, and it was indeed portrayed in early Christian iconography as a Tree of Life. The cross stood at the centre point of the world, Golgotha, the place where Adam, the first man, was buried. The blood of Christ dropped down onto the skull of Adam, revivifying him. The crucifixion of Jesus, as well as major episodes from Jesus' life, are interpreted in the New Testament within the context of temple symbols. The famous passage in Matthew 16:13–19 concerning the rock on which the church is built, against which the gates of hell will be impotent, can be related to Isaiah 28:16, 'I am laying a stone in Zion, a stone that has been tested, a precious cornerstone as a sure foundation.' Both refer to the Rock of Foundation in the Holy of Holies, which holds in place and caps the chaotic waters of the abyss. Jesus' reference in John 4:10 to the Samaritan woman about the 'living waters' that she will find by accepting him has meaning in the Old Testament concept of the 'living waters', or 'running waters', of Numbers 19:17, or the 'Fountain of Life' in Psalms 36:9.

The cross on which Jesus was crucified was portrayed in early Christian iconography as a Tree of Life ... and stood at the centre point of the world, where Adam, the first man, was buried.

Maya temples were viewed as sacred mountains, the doors of which were seen as the entryways into the caves at the heart of the holy mountain. Deep within the cave the Tree of the World grew, denoting the *axis mundi*, the centre place of the cosmos. This tree grew up out of the Maya underworld, Xibalba, and united all three of the main cosmic zones. A number of temples built together on a sacred platform thus represented a high mountain range, which towered over the tree stones on the floors of the plazas, representing a forest of trees. Sacred geography and sacred space then consisted of three elements: mountains, trees and caves.

→ In Christianity, the tree that bore the forbidden fruit in the Garden of Eden is sometimes identified with the tree of the cross. This wall-painting by Giovanni da Modena, c. 1420, shows Christ as the second Adam, redeeming the sins of the first.

THE inscriptions of the Sumerian king Gudea of Lagash place great emphasis on the temple as the *temen abzu*, the 'Foundation of the Abyss', or as the 'House of the Abyss', meaning that its foundations are sunk deep within the primordial waters, and rise up out of these waters. But there is another important aspect of the cosmology of the temple. Not only do creation and life come up out of the depths, *de profundis*, they come down from the sky, from the heavens, the classic dwelling place of the gods. The basic idea is that there exists in the sky a perfect place, the 'city' of the gods. The goal of human life is both to establish contact with this place, and to return to it after death, thus to share in the life of the gods. The primary way by which the gods share with humans the knowledge of this place, and information on how one gets there, is through the temple. The earthly temple is an exact replica of a heavenly temple.

The god reveals to a king, prophet or shaman the architectural plan for the earthly temple, which is a duplicate of the temple in heaven. Exodus chapters 19 and 25 give us the classic pattern: the prophet ascends the mountain. There, the prophet is given a 'pattern' to examine. That 'pattern' is the temple (or here, tabernacle, the prototype of the Israelite temple in Jerusalem) which exists in heaven: 'According to all that I show you concerning the pattern of the tabernacle and of all its furniture, so shall you make it' (Exodus 25:9).

The form of the White Dagoba in the Forbidden City in Beijing (*above*) is a large stupa, similar to the ones at Samye (*opposite*), and is symbolic of Mount Meru, the centre of the Buddhist universe. It is also a container for relics.

→ The layout of the 8th-century Tibetan Buddhist temple of Samye is a giant mandala – a pattern-like representation of the Buddhist universe and a tool for reaching enlightenment. Painting from the 18th or 19th century.

Likewise Ezekiel was 'brought ... in the visions of God into the land of Israel, and [set] down upon a very high mountain, on which was a structure like a city opposite me' (Ezekiel 40:2). Here the prophet was taken in visions in order to measure the Temple of Solomon in Jerusalem. A heavenly messenger guiding him held 'a measuring reed in his hand' (Ezekiel 40:3). We find a similar motif in the Book of Revelation, where the Apostle John was visited by an angel and 'In the Spirit ... carried ... away to a great, high mountain' (Revelation 21:10). The angel 'had a measuring rod of gold to measure the city and its gates and walls' (Revelation 21:15). John had been transported to the mountain in order to view the Heavenly city of Jerusalem, which in the context of the Book of Revelation was one vast temple.

The prophet is given a shaman-like vision on a mountain ... where he views the heavenly model in order to transfer its architecture to earth.

We see in both the Old and New Testament passages an important pattern, according to which the prophet is given a shaman-like vision on a mountain both prior to building the temple (where he views the heavenly model in order to transfer its architecture to the earth), and (as in the cases of Ezekiel and John), where he views either the temple or the heavenly temple-city prior to their *restoration* to the earth at the end of time.

The theme of the heavenly temple-city of Jerusalem, which at the end of time would be lowered down to earth, making of the entire earth one vast temple, persists throughout the Middle Ages, as can be seen in one of the illuminations to an early Spanish Beatus Apocalypse. There we see the plan view of the heavenly city, with John and the angel in the centre, the angel holding the golden measuring rod while John holds the book in which the revelations are recorded.

The earthly temple must incorporate features of the mountain. In India, a text states: 'Once heaven and earth were united. Let what is suitable to the sacrifice [namely, the temple] be common to both.' At Angkor the ancient Hindu cosmology of the central continent, Jambudvipa, encircled by six rings of mountain ranges, with seven oceans, and at the very centre, the world mountain Meru, was exactly reproduced during the ninth to twelfth centuries AD. The world of the gods was brought down to the world of humans, bringing the two into the contact that assured that prosperity and life would flow from the gods to humans, through the presence and ritual of the temples.

The Kaabah in Mecca, Islam's holiest shrine, is seen as the exact image of the heavenly throne or temple, and is thus the centre of the terrestrial world. The architecture of the heavenly model descended onto the earth, taking the form of the straight sides of the earthly temple (the cube-shaped Kaabah), symbolizing the possibility of direct communication between heaven and earth.

Of all temple-building cultures of the world, the peoples of the Valley of Mexico were most profoundly influenced in their temple ritual and architecture by cosmic concepts. The pyramid-temple complexes of Maya cities reproduced on earth the sacred landscape created by the gods at the beginning of time. The Pyramid of the Sun, the central pyramid in the Avenue of the Dead complex at Teotihuacán (known anciently as 'the place where man becomes divine'), dates to the Maya Classic Period. It was constructed according to an extensive astronomical symbolism. The pyramid was built over a previous shrine, which in turn was built over a subterranean cave that had long been the centre for cult practices. The cave itself was a seven-pronged chamber which figures in the Maya creation account, the *Popol Vuh*, as the place where the ancestors first emerged (the Aztecs later buried their rulers in this cave). The earthly city was seen as the exact mirror image of the heavenly city, with the major axis – the Avenue of the Dead – and the

---

In ancient Egypt and Mesopotamia, the Bible, and Mesoamerica, the king was pre-eminently a builder, a builder of temples. The plan of the temple could only come to him through contact with the sacred ...

---

temples and pyramids built along that axis oriented astronomically to the Pleiades, the four cardinal directions, and the surrounding mountains. The numerous platforms situated along the Avenue of the Dead are actually connected more with the universe through the cosmic orientation than with each other as parts of a more traditional architectural arrangement. The cave directly underneath the Pyramid of the Sun was illuminated by the sun each year at the summer solstice. Here we see the two main concepts that have been emphasized above: the sacred place rising up out of the underworld, the place from which life comes, and its architectural plan brought down out of the heavens.

The Maya Temple of the Inscriptions in Palenque, from the 7th century AD. Cut into the ground underneath it is an intricate vaulted crypt where the Maya king Pacal is buried.

In ancient Egypt and Mesopotamia, in the Bible, and in Mesoamerica, the king was pre-eminently a builder, a builder of temples. The plan of the temple could only come to him through contact with the sacred, either through direct revelation, or through fundamental grounding, plus initiation, in the sacred texts and traditions. The famous statue of King Gudea of Lagash shows him holding on his lap the lapis lazuli plan of the temple that had been revealed to him in a dream during his night in a temple (*pp. 108–9*).

Thus, in the ancient temple-building societies, order did not exist, the earth was not cosmicized, society did not function properly, the law codes could not be decreed, except in a temple established on earth that was the authentic and divinely revealed counterpart of a heavenly prototype.

SACRED GEOMETRY

BY sacred geometry we mean a mathematics that had as its purpose the accurate laying out of the temple ground plan in relation to the cardinal directions and to the heavens; in other words, the ritually proper and absolutely accurate transferral of the heavenly plan onto the earth. The temple is the reduced plan of the cosmos, and as such must be an accurate representation of the heavenly prototype. Accuracy is vitally important. A wrong orientation would bring death, destruction and all manner of disasters.

The temple is the reduced plan of the cosmos, and as such must be an accurate representation of the heavenly prototype.

All of these considerations made the actual preparation of the site and laying of the foundations actions that were immersed in ritual. Chief among these was the 'stretching of the cord', well attested in both ancient Egypt and India, a kind of 'sacred surveying', which established the ground plan of the building, set its four corners – oriented to the cardinal directions – and brought the earthly building into relationship with the gods of the heavens and the constellations, or the gods in their guise as constellations.

The ritual of stretching the cord is known in Egypt from as early as the Second Dynasty king Khasekhemwy to as late as the Ptolemaic Period Temple of Edfu (built between 237 and 57 BC). The astronomical ceiling from the unfinished tomb of Senmut at Deir el-Bahri (about 1458 BC) gives a fascinatingly clear view of the astronomical underpinnings of this rite. The rite continued virtually unchanged over several thousand years, and in fact the Edfu texts state that the ritual of stretching the cord originated with the legendary architect, sage, physician and magician, Imhotep of the reign of Djoser (Third Dynasty).

→ The inscribed columns and inner sanctum of the Temple of Horus at Edfu. The temple itself is said to be built on the location of a cosmic battle between the gods Horus and Seth.

The pharaoh and the goddess Seshat determine the location for a temple in the ceremonial stretching of the cord. Egyptian relief from Edfu.

In the Egyptian ritual, which took place during the night, at the time of the new moon, the sky was first 'stretched out', its ultimate boundaries determined and set out with particular reference to the constellation known in Egyptian as *Mshtjw*. The goddess Seshat, 'Mistress of the ground plans and the writings', 'Lady of plans, Lady of writings in the House of Life', working together with the king, acting as the son of god, as Horus, and also with Thoth, god of the ground plans and the construction prescriptions, led in the surveying procedures.

On a night of the new moon, when *Mshtjw* (Ursa Major) could be observed, the heavens were laid out. At the same time, still during the night, the surveying cord was stretched out over the temple site, establishing the four corners of the building. In the tomb of Senmut, two transit lines extend across the northern part of the ceiling, and attach themselves to the lower portion of *Mshtjw*. These lines have been interpreted as a visual representation of the process of sighting on the circumpolar stars, and have been associated with a well-known 'stretching of the cord' text, which states, in part, 'I have grasped the peg ... I observe the forward-striding movement of the constellations. My eye is fixed on the Great Bear. I ... determine the corners of your temple' (quoted in S. Giedion, *The Beginnings of Architecture*).

With the passing of the night and the rising of the sun god, Re, the chaos of the dark but starry night is overcome, and cosmos is established ...

This text is found at the Edfu temple, and forms a part of the construction texts found in the main shrine and on the exterior of the enclosure wall. With the passing of the night and the rising of the sun god, Re, the chaos of the dark but starry night is overcome, and cosmos is established, cosmos that consists of the coordination of the heavens with the earth, centred in the earthly temple.

In another Egyptian example of this ritual, the texts accompanying the relief scenes in the temple of Seti I, at Abydos (about 1305–1290 BC), show the king and Sefkhet-'Abwy (as Seshat was known at that period), laying out the temple foundation lines before Osiris. The text has Sefkhet-'Abwy saying: 'It is Ptah who lays out its foundations in person; it is thy father Re who establishes it like his horizon.' Osiris then says: 'I cause thy mansion to abide like the sky.' The scene is titled 'Stretching the cord in the Mansion of Usimare-setepenre [the Prenomen of Ramesses II, the son of Seti I, and the finisher of this temple], near to the necropolis.'

Tibetan mandalas are drawn out on the ground according to the most minutely detailed ritual instructions. The initial lines are laid down with a white cord. For the subsequent lines, five threads (sutra) of the finest quality, each of a different colour and twisted together, are dipped in coloured powder. The cord (called 'the cord of gnosis') is then stretched out along the ground, demarcating the line of the mandala. When the cord has been stretched taut, it is raised up and allowed to fall suddenly, leaving a residue of coloured powder to form the proper line on the ground. This procedure is repeated numerous times, until the general outlines of the mandala are achieved. All aspects of the cord-stretching ceremonies are described in the Tibetan treatises in extreme detail, including the lengths of the cord, purification rituals, and so on. The five cords represent the five Buddha families (detailed below in connection with Borobudur). The central axis of the mandala, representing the *axis mundi*, Mount Meru, is drawn by a cord called 'Thread of Brahma', which is used to establish the median north to south and east to west lines.

In India, the temple was always built only after observing the stars for favourable configurations. The images of the regents of the planets and the stars were carved into the walls of the temple. Indeed, the very plan of the Indian temple, the *Vastupurusamandala*, had represented on it the thirty-two *Naksatras*, the constellations that the moon passes through on its monthly course. The astrologer consulted these at every stage in the temple building: the determination of the purification of the soil, the insemination of the ground, the levelling of the site, the determination of the cosmic orientation of the building, the construction and placing of the altar, and the stretching of the cord as the mandala was laid out on the ground; in each case determinations were made according to the place of the sun, the moon, or one of the planets within the circle of the heavenly bodies that were represented on the sacred ground plan.

In Egypt, temple sites were given magical protection through a rite of circumambulation by the gods, in which statues or images for all gods for whom the temple was being built were carried around the site, clockwise. Circumambulation is a ritual act that commemorates the journey of the sun god through the heavens, and thus further cosmicizes the building.

→ The Bayon temple at Angkor, Cambodia, was built by Jayavarman VII in the late 12th century. Monumental faces look out over the four quarters of the temple dedicated to the Buddha.

Perhaps no temple complex has ever been so thoroughly and minutely oriented to the heavenly bodies as Angkor Wat, built by Suryavarman II over a thirty-year period during the early 12th century AD. Recent exhaustive astronomical studies conducted at the site and published in *Science* have shown that the temple entrances, which, in contrast to other temples in Cambodia, were constructed facing west, ensured that the rising sun was directly aligned across the topmost tower precisely at the entrance on the equinox and solstice days (which correlates with the worship of the sun god Vishnu by the builder, King Suryavarman II, who died in 1150). Altogether, twenty-two positions within the temple were used to observe the sun and the moon. Most astonishing of all, the east–west axis of the temple recorded, in architectural distances, both the passing of the 365-day year, and the four major periods (yugas) of Hindu cosmology: the Krita, Treta, Dvapara and Kali yugas. Furthermore, the two worst and most degenerate yugas, Kali and Dvapara, were arranged along the axis so that they were the farthest in distance from the main shrine of the temple, which is nestled inside the base of the central tower that represents the central peak of Mount Meru, the centre and axis of the universe.

The rocky peaks of Angkor Wat represent Mount Meru, the mid-point of the cosmos.

Various traditions within Islam give two complementary accounts of the building of the Kaabah in Mecca. In the first of these, a tent from among the tents in Paradise is lowered onto the earth, fitting exactly the space into which the Kaabah was constructed. In various traditions the tent is put into place by the Angel Gabriel, other angels, or by God himself. The tent is fastened with four pegs of gold, symbolizing universal nature in its four-fold division. The ropes of the tent were of silken thread as fine as hair, and were violet in colour, representing the emanations of the Light of the Soul. The tent's central pillar was of red hyacinth. Red was taken to be a combination of white (the dimension of Light) and black (the dimension of Darkness), thus symbolizing the Divine, which intermingles the duality of light and darkness.

Perhaps no temple complex has ever been so thoroughly and minutely oriented to the heavenly bodies as Angkor Wat, built over a thirty-year period during the early 12th century AD.

According to the second tradition, Adam was taken to the site of the Kaabah by the Angel Gabriel, carrying with him the Black Stone. Upon their arrival at the site, a white cloud descended from heaven and enveloped them. Gabriel commanded Adam to trace with his foot a groove in the earth that corresponded exactly to the shadow cast by the cloud. This became the exact outline of the Kaabah. Gabriel then instructed Adam to continue tracing the outline of the heavenly cloud, and this became the precincts of the sacred *haram*, the area that surrounds the Kaabah. The Black Stone was then desposited in the north-east corner, as a symbol of the heavenly compact made between God and his creatures, and it was on this spot that the sons of Adam brought their sacrifice to God.

The role of sacred geometry in Maya temples of the Petén region in Guatemala has been extensively documented. Many such temples were constructed for geomantic purposes, with elaborate sight lines on the sun, moon or stars. Of particular importance are the three Group E temples at Uaxactún, north of Tikal. Here, three small temples stood on a north–south axis across a courtyard from a pyramid facing east. These temples marked the solstice and equinox cycles of the sun. From the pyramid steps the sun arose directly over the central temple on the equinoxes, over the southernmost on the winter solstice and the northernmost at the summer solstice. Such arrangements were meant to reflect the cosmic order in the arrangement of the courtyards, with their temples and platforms, the entire ensemble connected with the heavens by means of astronomical sight lines.

→ An aerial view of the Maya temples at Tikal. The back of Temple I, the Temple of the Great Jaguar, can be seen in the foreground of the photograph; it faces the three-stepped pyramid of Temple II in the Great Plaza.

At Tikal, Maya ideas of solar cycles and other calendric information were incorporated into the architecture of the building.

At Tikal, also in the Petén region (built in the Maya Classic Period), the Temple of the Great Jaguar (Temple I), on the eastern side of the Great Plaza, was built in nine architectural levels, expressing the Maya view of the nine underworld regions. Maya ideas of solar cycles and other calendric information were incorporated into the architecture of the building. In the same complex at Tikal there are ceremonial complexes consisting of twin platforms with stairs on four sides, facing each other at the east and west ends of a temenos. Since there are no temples on top of the platforms, they may have served for ritual performances or sacred dance within the temple complex. There are nine monolithic stelae in front of the west platform, with a round altar in front of each stela. A long building on the northern edge of the temenos has nine doors. These 'twin complexes' were built to commemorate a *katun*, a sacred calendric cycle of twenty years.

Among the Germanic peoples a sacred pole, the Irminsul, was thought to hold up the heavens and was considered to be the cosmic world pillar. Charlemagne destroyed the Irminsul and sacred woods of the temple in Erisburg in AD 772. According to Rudolph of Fulda (c. 860), this column was the 'column of the universe holding up almost all things'. Sometimes such pillars would be tilted towards the north, thus representing the axis of the universe. The pillar on the earth was a model of the pillar in heaven, thus the heavenly spheres revolved around the earthly temple. Nails would be driven into the column, representing the Pole Star, and it was along this column that the shaman ascended into heaven. With this central pillar in place, uniting the world regions (the pillar also extends to the underworld) the prophet or king or shaman could also enter the temple at night in order to have numinous dreams. Thus Gudea of Lagash entered the temple, where he received a message through a dream that he was to build a temple to the god Ningirsu.

The combination of the central pillar and the dream come together in the dream that Jacob had at Bethel (Genesis 28). He slept on the primordial stone, the place where creation on earth was carried out by God. During his sleep Jacob dreamt of a ladder 'set up on the earth, and the top of it reached to heaven; and behold, the angels of God were ascending and descending on it' (Genesis 28:12). God then gave him the message that 'the land on which you lie I will give to you and to your descendants' (13). The ladder is the prototype of the pillar which unites heaven and earth. Upon awakening Jacob was overcome with the awesomeness of the place, and exclaimed: 'This is none other than the house of God, and this is the gate of Heaven' (17). He then designated the place as Beth El, Bethel, the House of God (i.e. the temple) (22).

Jacob's ladder depicted in stone on 16th-century Bath Abbey, England. Uniquely in architecture, the west side of the building represents the church itself as the ladder to salvation.

The ceiling of the ambulatory in the Dome of the Rock, Jerusalem, is embellished with intricate geometric patterns.

It was the custom among the ancient Sumerians and their predecessors in Iraq to incorporate the foundations of crumbling temples into new structures, thus incorporating the sanctity and numinous power of the previous temple. The old building would be filled in with mud bricks, then levelled off, providing a building platform on which the new temple would rise. This process is documented in the temple precinct at the site of Eridu, the first Sumerian city, and at Uruk and other cities, for over one thousand years during the Ubaid and Uruk Periods. The great majority of Classical Greek temples were founded on the remains of earlier Mycenaean temples. The Temple Mount of Jerusalem, where the Dome of the Rock stands today, has a tradition as a sacred temenos going back at least four thousand years. According to the Old Testament accounts, the place where Abraham (about 2000 BC) was commanded to sacrifice Isaac was the sacred high place, Mount Moriah. This same place was the threshing floor that David (about 1000 BC) bought from Araunah the Jebusite, 'in order to build an altar to the Lord' (2 Samuel 24:21). The threshing floor in the ancient world carried the symbolism of the omphalos, or the navel of the world, thus an emblem of the universe (a round piece of earth, with the axis in the middle, with the oxen of the sun going around it). This then became the place where Solomon erected the Temple of the Lord (after about 960 BC), 'His holy mountain, beautiful in elevation' (Psalms 48:2).

47

THE MANDALA

THE primary expression of sacred geometry in temple architecture is the mandala. The mandala is a sacred, numinous shape consisting of the intersection of a circle (the shape of the heavens) and a square (the primary shape on the earth's surface). Mandalas have been called 'graphic mirrors of supernatural essences' and 'maps of the cosmos'. By their very nature they cosmicize a building constructed to be a temple, and establish that building as the centre, with the world-tree at its axis, uniting the three main levels of the universe and sanctifying the four world regions.

The mandala is a sacred, numinous shape consisting of the intersection of a circle (the shape of the heavens) and a square (the primary shape on the earth's surface). Mandalas have been called 'graphic mirrors of supernatural essences', and 'maps of the cosmos'.

But it goes beyond the architectural, and particularly in Tantric Buddhism, is transferred or projected onto the human body, where all the features of the painted or architectural mandala are represented at the appropriate places in the body, the chakras. Furthermore, in Tantrism, the mandala is the focal point of meditation techniques. No actual or visible mandala need be present as the initiate experiences the journey to enlightenment in the mind, all the architectural details of the mandala are present in the visualization process. This is expressed in one text as follows: 'The body becomes a [mandala] palace, the hallowed basis of all the Buddhas' (Wayman). In this sense, the mandala becomes what has been called a psychocosmogram. A sand or coloured-powder mandala can sanctify the place, however secular may be its basic purpose and use, as, for example, in the Paramount Theatre in Madison Square Garden in New York City, during October 1991. Rituals were carried out that prepared the auditorium for initiation ceremonies, and as a result it became 'the sacred mandala palace of Kalachakra', with the initiate visualizing himself seated at the eastern door.

→ A Kalachakra mandala painting from Tibet. Rectangles inside circles and the surrounding deities enable the initiate to focus the mind and, with practice, to attain enlightenment.

The basic ground plan of the Hindu temple is founded on a mandala that bears the name *Vastupurusamandala*. The component parts of this Sanskrit word, and their meanings, are: *vastu*, 'that which exists in an ordered state'; *purusa*, 'universal, supernal, or cosmic man (the unconditioned self)'; and *mandala*, 'the numinous shape'. The *Vastupurusamandala* is square, because in India the square is the paramount, perfect shape, signifying order, finality and perfection. The circle emanates from the square, is thus derivative from it, and signifies growth and movement. The circle symbolizes our present world, the square the perfect world of the heavens. The round earth and the square heaven are joined by the four cardinal directions, primarily east and west, the places of the rising and setting sun, where the earth and heaven come closest together. Thus, the earth and sky themselves, in their union, form a mandala.

Borobudur is perhaps the most magnificent example of sacred architecture in the world ... It encompasses everything that we can posit of temple architecture, symbol and ritual.

The most extraordinary architectural expression of a mandala is the temple of Borobudur, in the centre of Java. Borobudur, perhaps the most magnificent example of sacred architecture in the world, was built during the eighth and ninth centuries by the Buddhist Sailendra dynasty. Borobudur encompasses everything that we can posit of temple architecture, symbol and ritual. It is at once a mountain, and a magnificent mandala of the Tantric (esoteric) type well known in Tibet and Nepal.

Borobudur is a sacred site, an object of pilgrimage, a symbolic mountain, an allegory of progress through rising terraces to divine revelation and an exposition in stone to a whole theological doctrine.

Borobudur stands in the Kedu Plain in central Java, south of a line of volcanoes, each of which are over 3,000 metres (10,000 ft) high. Its intimate relationship to the volcanoes can be seen in the etymology of the name of the ruling family that built the monument – Sailendra, 'Lords of the Mountain'. It appears to have been constructed away from any major city, and fits beautifully the pattern of a pilgrimage mountain-temple (in a natural paradise). There is evidence that Chinese pilgrims continued to visit the site even after it had been abandoned locally and Javanese civilization had shifted further to the east of the island. Its famous plan, widely illustrated, is probably the best-known mandala configuration in the world.

Borobudur is a structure with a square base, oriented towards the four cardinal directions, and with four monumental staircases in the middle of each face. Six lower levels are square, with returns and projections, while there are four upper, circular terraces, the topmost of which supports the central stupa. Each staircase goes all the way to the topmost terrace. Of the six lower terraces, the middle four consist of galleries with relief sculptures, which completely enclose the pilgrim on both sides, but are open to the sky. The base of the lowest level was decorated with reliefs showing the underworld 'hell worlds', but these are no longer visible, except for one section in the so-called 'hidden foot'.

The galleries were meant to be circumambulated in a clockwise direction, so that the initiate could observe and 'read' the reliefs, which gradually took them to ever greater spiritual heights.

The galleries were meant to be circumambulated in a clockwise direction (*pradakshina*), so that the initiate could observe and 'read' the reliefs, which gradually took them to ever greater spiritual heights as they gradually circumambulated and ascended to the higher levels. Within each gallery, the outer balustrade wall contains two levels of reliefs, while the inner or gallery wall contains one level. The entire series is a continuous narrative, consisting of tales and stories from the previous lives of the Buddha, his earthly life, and stories of previous Buddhas. From the second to the fourth galleries, the reliefs recount the spiritual wanderings of the pilgrim Sudhana, who sought out numerous teachers in his quest to become a bodhisattva, and who finally, as depicted at the end of the series of reliefs in the fourth gallery, gained entrance into the palace of the Buddha-to-be, Maitreya,on Mount Sumeru.

The first three upper, circular terraces contain 72 stupas, 32 on the first circular level, 24 on the second, and 16 on the third. The *anda*, or domical section of each stupa, was constructed with stone lattice work, so that one can see the inside of the dome. The stupas on the two lower circular levels have diamond-shaped lattice work, with square *harmikas* (the altar on top of the dome), while those on the third level show square lattice work and octagonal *harmikas*. Each of the stupas contained a seated Buddha figure, his hands forming a mudra

As each worshipper rises up through Borobudur, he or she must pass detailed stone friezes depicting the lives of the Buddha on earth.

(gesture) which has been variously identified as *dharmachakra* (turning of the wheel of law) or *bodhyangi-mudra* (member of enlightenment). Each Buddha could be seen through the lattice work. The topmost stupa originally contained a Buddha figure (later stolen), which some scholars believe was of the Adibuddha, hidden within the dome of the structure and thus out of view to pilgrims. The Adibuddha is the primordial Buddha, the primal, non-dual essence, the source of universal mind, from which everything emanates, that is, from which the physical universe originates. Adibuddha is unborn and uncreated, exists spontaneously, without cause or dependent origination, and yet is the ultimate cause and originator of everything in the universe.

On the lower, gallery levels, five balustrades are formed that look out over the plain in each direction. Seated within niches ranged along each balustrade, facing the four directions, are, in total, 432 Buddhas. The Buddhas on each side of the temple on the first four balustrades all sit in the same posture, with the same mudra. Those on the east sit in *bhumisparsa*, 'touching the earth', and represent the *dhyani* or meditation Buddha Akshobhya; those on the south make the gesture of *varada*, 'greeting', corresponding to the Dhyani Buddha Ratnasambhava; the Buddhas on the west side sit with the mudra of *dhyani*, 'meditation', and represent Amitabha; while those on the north face of the monument express the gesture of *abhaya-mudra*, 'fearlessness', the mudra of the Dhyani Buddha Amoghasiddhi. The sixty-four Buddhas in the niches of the fifth balustrade level all form the same mudra in each direction, *vitarka-mudra*, 'teaching', and represent the Dhyani Buddha Vairocana. The total number of Buddhas in the niches along the balustrades is 432, one of the most important numinous numbers within the Indian religious tradition, symbolizing a *mahayuga*, 4,320,000 human years, the total time of the four world ages: Krita Yuga, Treta Yuga, Dvapara Yuga and Kali Yuga.

← Mount Kailash in the Himalayas is seen as the earthly manifestation of Mount Meru. The object of one of the most devout and flourishing pilgrimages in the world, the mountain stands for spiritual progress.

The Buddhas in the niches of the four faces have the appearance, from a distance, of siddhas, or hermits, meditating deep within caves on the sides of the sacred mountain. The circumambulating initiate would rise ever higher up the holy mountain, learning the sacred doctrines through the reliefs, ascending through the world as we know it, to the level of inner vision, of meditation, leaving the world of appearances, and reaching, as it were, the foothills of Mount Meru, in the Himalayan range. This is not the highest, formless, state of existence, because he can still see (though with some difficulty through the lattice work) the meditating Buddhas inside the stupas. Finally, he would reach the level of the topmost stupa, the summit of the cosmic mountain, Mount Meru, within which the essence of all existence, the Adibuddha, symbolizing formlessness and emptiness, sat, but out of view to the human eye. This would have been at the exact centre of the topmost, domical stupa, at the axis of the world mountain, and thus of the universe.

Borobudur has been placed within the context of the Tibetan and Nepalese Tantric traditions of Diamond World Mandalas, which have their architectural expression in the Himalayan regions in the so-called Adibuddha Stupas, the most famous example of which is the Kumbum Temple at Gyantse, in Tibet. Kumbum, built about five hundred years later than Borobudur, has virtually the same top plan as Borobudur, although its upper, circular terraces are, in typical Tibetan style, domical, not open. In this conception the Adibuddha, the formless, non-dual centre and source of all emanation, is seen at work at each level of the temple-mountain: the hell worlds, the form realms of earthly existence, and in his manifestations as the five Dhyani Buddhas, who represent the five-fold transcendent wisdom of the Adibuddha.

The five Dhyani Buddhas have each presided over a world system. The pilgrim or initiate comes to the temple to learn the essence of a vast cosmic world-system (for example, the role of the measurement of the Kalpas in temples such as Angkor Wat and Borobudur), and thus ultimately about creation itself. One learns also the insubstantiality of all appearance.

The mandala as an expression of sacred geometry is deeply rooted in the architecture of early Christian churches. This can be seen most vividly in the vault directly over the main altar at San Vitale in Ravenna (dedicated in AD 547). Much of the symbolism of the temple comes together in the magnificent mosaic (p. 110). Jesus, represented as the Lamb of God, stands at the centre of the mandala configuration, which represents the starry night sky as well as the celestial Church. Four angels hold up the vault of heaven, with the Lamb in the centre, surrounded by stars, representing resurrection. The heavenly tabernacle is filled with plants and animals that are reminiscent of the pristine paradise, the place of first creation, that is so often represented in the architecture or painted illustration of the temple.

➤ Borobudur's fearsome gargoyles channel rainwater down to the base. This one is from around 830.

RITUAL

TO benefit from the temple ordinary mortals must approach it with great care. The temple is a dynamo, a place of considerable power. The numinous is both life-giving and dangerous. Ordinary mortals, indeed priests too, approach the temple through ancient, carefully prescribed ritual preparations, including purification, special clothing, certain ritual movements and gestures (mudra), ritual speech (mantra), visual symbols (yantra) and group interaction. These rituals are not something recently thought up or devised in popular religious or artistic movements (although traditional forms of ritual may well appear in these media). They bear the stamp of tradition, are often passed on by elderly members of a society, are usually considered to be secret, and are purposefully kept from the knowledge of outsiders, or those who have not been initiated.

Ritual is the primary means that makes communication possible between humans and the powers beyond immediate human life – the transcendent.

Ritual is the primary means that makes communication possible between humans and the powers beyond immediate human life – the transcendent. Ritual is the process through which contact with the world of the numinous powers is activated. It is not something dry, ossified, or meaningless, as it is widely thought to be in the Western world. It is a means of access to spiritual power.

→ Common to all temples is the conviction that a divine person is literally present within them. In this part of a Flemish diptych by Christian de Hondt, 1499, oversized figures of the Virgin Mary and child are shown inside a church.

A 15th-century scroll painting of Nichiren, a Japanese sect leader, searching for a temple site. Only the authorized master, who has received his knowledge from tradition, can find the correct site for a temple, as it is he alone who can communicate with higher forces.

One simply does not and cannot approach the transcendent powers casually. And one cannot make up one's own agenda in communicating with such powers. One must look to the past, to the written tradition, and to the authorized masters who have received such knowledge through oral tradition. These traditions can only be kept alive by ongoing communication between humans and the transcendent, through a living ritual tradition – in the temple.

The means of approach and of arrival are what we understand in the term 'ritual'. Even where we speak of 'the temple built without hands', in other words the 'psychocosmogram' such as the interior mandala, or the interior Kabbalistic tradition, a master teacher – a guru – is needed to guide the initiate.

Within the Tibetan tradition of Secret Mantra Vajrayana Buddhism three assumptions are made about initiation: 1) the hall or room where the initiation is taking place is the Pure Realm; 2) the lama directing the initiation is the Primordial Buddha; 3) the initiates are receiving secret oral teachings. The etymology of the Tibetan word for 'initiation' is 'conferral of power'. At the beginning of each teaching or initiation within Tibetan Buddhism the lama conducting the ceremony recites to the initiates his own 'chain of authority', going into great detail, and tracing the authority back to the Buddha himself. It is such authority that makes possible, as I mentioned above, the transformation of the Paramount Theatre in New York City into the 'Mandala Palace of Kalachakra'.

Thus, ritual is not a casual new invention. It is as old as the temple itself, and must be carefully followed, lest harm result. I am not talking here about forms of customary or oft-repeated human behaviour, such as walking the dog in the same direction each morning and buying the morning paper at exactly the same time – actions that many speak of as 'ritual'. I am referring to religious liturgies in which every detail of the performance is specified, and opportunities for variation are narrowly limited.

Knowledge of this ritual is the secret, esoteric tradition that is kept in the temple libraries as books, manuscripts or in some other written form, and that is passed on orally, as a secret doctrine by acknowledged teachers and masters.

A Tibetan mandala painting illustrating the concept of the temple descending to a group of priests. The secrets of the temple, only revealed to those initiates in the inner circle, are passed down from the heavenly sphere by an angel.

But if information on the secret tradition is contained in books, can one not learn about this tradition simply by reading such books, many of which are widely published and accessible today? The answer is no. This is evident if one compares, say, the *Kalachakra Tantra Rite of Initiation*, edited and translated by Jeffrey Hopkins, with the actual initiation ceremony. There is much that occurs during the ceremony that would not be understood by one who had only read the book. The initiation must be experienced under the guidance of an authorized master, who administers oaths and gives instructions, many of which belong to the secret, oral tradition, and are accompanied by information not otherwise available to the uninitiated.

The emphasis on authority figures and on the great age of rituals does not mean that innovations do not occur. But when they do occur, the change takes place within the context of the authority structure, and the changes would not be so drastic that the resultant rituals would be unrecognizable to adherents. Within modern, technological society we value change, and are used to yearly change in many customs and technologies. But in the great religious traditions, change is viewed with suspicion, especially if it is imposed from outside the traditional authority structures.

Some ritual is related to the shape of the sacred mountain, or to the sphericity of the heavens, or the course of the sun. These three could provide a partial explanation for one of the most basic ritual movements, circumambulation, which is present in most of the ritual of world religion. Circumambulation represents totality, perfection and taking inner, spiritual possession.

As in many other cultures, processions and rituals marked the sacred festivals in ancient Greece. Here a lively cavalry parade is depicted in a relief, c. 440 BC, from the Parthenon.

Another common type of ritual movement is to walk upward, which can be related to the journey up the sacred mountain. A third is to walk inward, to the interior of the sanctuary, where the most holy place is to be found. These three important types of ritual movement can all be seen in the ritual journey of the initiate at Borobudur: circumambulating

Ritual dancing in a group setting was a way of forming social bonds, both within the temple and in society. In this funeral dance, illustrated in a painting from a 4th-century BC Etruscan tomb, the interlinked arms of the participants are symbolic of the unity of life and death.

Circumambulation is one of the most basic ritual movements ... it represents totality, perfection and taking inner, spiritual possession.

the galleries, ascending in height at each new gallery, moving ever inward towards the centre of the mountain-temple. Thus one walks around, upward and inward, to the centre. In Egyptian temples, each successive threshold rose to a higher level, until one reached the highest elevation in the back of the temple, in the inner sanctum, representing the primordial mound of creation.

Other forms that ritual movement may take include dance, speech and vigorous body movement, all of which, with some exceptions, take place within a group setting, since temple ritual is one of the most powerful social bonding mechanisms in traditional societies. Ritual is related to the establishment of a harmonious society through group interaction and celebration of stages in the human and natural life cycle, and observation of the calendric cycle of festivals. The kinds of movement, and of preparation, such as purification, changing of clothes, and so forth, that come to be required in order to approach a temple, are canonized, and, once canonized, persist through many generations and become very widespread geographically.

Ritual is related to the establishment of a harmonious society through group interaction and celebration of stages in the human and natural life cycle, and observation of the calendric cycle of festivals.

Greek drama has been thought to have originated in the initiation rites dedicated to Dionysus. The central feature of the Dionysiac and Orphic rites at such shrines as Delphi, Eleusis and Agrae was the worshipper's belief that he could actually become one with and share the destiny of Dionysus or Orpheus, just as in Egypt initiates shared the destiny of Osiris, and in Christianity the destiny of Christ. There was a strong pantomimic element in the Dionysiac cults, in which initiates played the roles of various deities in the cycle of dramatic stories revolving around that deity. The end result of the rituals was that the initiate would overcome the effects of death. Plutarch consoled his wife upon the death of their young daughter by telling her that she should remember 'the mystic symbols of the rites of initiation to Dionysus'.

The omphalos or navel of the world, the primordial tumulus stone, symbol of the Earth Mother and of Dionysus, was also a centrepiece of the rituals at Delphi, Agrae and Eleusis. Here the initiate came, dancing the ecstatic ritual dance before the omphalos, on which Greek vase paintings depict Dionysus seated. Initiation thus centred on the supreme oracle, the seat of life and of revelation of the mysteries of death and of the world beyond.

→ In this architecturally accurate drawing of Delphi sculptures and buildings stand on the side of the hill but the Temple of Apollo dominates the view. Ceremonies and purification rituals would have been performed as pilgrims made their journey up the sacred way.

Within Islam, the primary ritual action of the Pilgrimage – circumambulation seven times around the Kaabah – originates in Heaven. Just as in Heaven the angels walk around the Divine Throne, so on earth human beings walk around the earthly model of the Heavenly Throne. Just as the earthly temple is based on a heavenly archetype, so also is earthly ritual based on heavenly ritual. The number seven is archetypal, representing the seven millennia of earthly existence, as well as the seventy thousand angels who surround the Heavenly Throne, the seven divine attributes, and the seven veils that separate God from humankind. Ritual thus also partakes of sacred geometry. What exactly does circumambulation represent in esoteric Islam, other than being a pattern of heavenly action? It is a process of taking possession of totality, of encircling, encompassing, as well as being encompassed by, universal intelligence. It signifies the restoration within oneself of the White Pearl, restored from the Black Stone, restoring within oneself the celestial body of light which originates in the heavenly realms and is to be found in the earthly model of the celestial, the Kaabah.

The ancient peoples who painted shrines such as these at Lascaux, France, would have had to undertake a treacherous journey in order to reach a suitable place to make the painting.

← It is every Muslim's duty to complete a pilgrimage to Mecca once in his or her lifetime. At this unique focus of Islamic devotion, worshippers must circumambulate the Kaabah seven times.

Erich Neumann called ritual 'the archetype of the way'. The earliest 'way' into the centre that is recorded in human experience, he believed, is to be found in the Upper Paleolithic caves of Europe. Fundamental to the cave shrines of Laussel, Pech Merle, and Lascaux was the dark, dangerous journey into the deep interior of the caves, where the shrines were created and the wall paintings executed. From these early experiences, Neumann proposed, came concepts of ritual that are still with us today. Underlying all temple ritual is the idea of the mysteries that are preserved there, and of the difficult, labyrinthine journey of initiation that one must take to reach the centre. Furthermore, one needs a leader, a teacher, one who has already experienced the danger of the way since he has himself been initiated. The prototypes of these concepts Neumann found in the Upper Paleolithic caves, with the dark, dangerous journey one would have had to take to reach the interior, and the mysteries of the Great Mother that originated there.

THE mysteries of the temple take many forms, differing from culture to culture, and are in fact in many ways culture specific, as we would expect. Two types of temple initiation, however, are particularly widespread, and these are the 'theatrical' staging of ritual performances based on the creation myths, and the initiation of the living into the knowledge and mysteries of the afterlife.

Already in 1867 the great pioneer of Egyptology, Lepsius, wrote: 'The *Book of the Dead*, or the collection of the texts relating to the resurrection, the judgment, and the life in the other world, was in its essential character a book of practical instruction. Its aim was to inform the individual, intent on his spiritual welfare, about what already on earth should be known and prepared by him for his death'.

Two types of temple initiation are particularly widespread, these are the 'theatrical' staging of ritual performances based on the creation myths, and the initiation of the living into the knowledge and mysteries of the afterlife.

Thus, creation and death were the two grand themes, and it was these that informed the ritual processes of the temples and benefited the relative few who could actually gain access to them. The best-known example from ancient Egypt of a ritual drama based on a creation text is the so-called 'Theology of Memphis', the famous Shabaka Stone. Pharaoh Shabaka (716–702 BC) of the Twenty-fifth Dynasty discovered an ancient text in a temple in Memphis, a text relating the creation according to the traditions of Memphis, and its chief god, Ptah. The text gives solid evidence that it was meant to be performed, with actors (usually thought to have been priests) taking the parts of the various deities and speaking the parts assigned to them, for example, 'Words spoken by Geb to Seth', and 'Words spoken by Geb to Horus'. The story was recited and explained to the ancient audience by a lector priest.

➡ Image of a shrine to Osiris, the god of the afterlife, from the Egyptian *Book of the Dead*. Behind the seated Osiris is his wife and sister, Isis, the goddess of motherhood and nature; in front of him is a fetish to Anubis, a symbol of embalming.

Some of the few surviving stone pillars from the Temple of Osiris at Abydos, where mysterious processions and rites – both public and solely for priests – dedicated to this lord of the underworld would have taken place.

Another Egyptian text, the stela of Ikhernofret, an official of the Twelfth Dynasty, records his visit upstream, at the behest of King Senwosret III, to take part in the mystery rites of Osiris at Abydos. He mentions roles that he played in the drama ('I acted as the "Son-Whom-He-Loves" for Osiris' – that is, he played the role of Horus, the son of Osiris). He refers to ritual actions that occurred during the play: 'I opposed those rebellious to the *neshmet*-barque, and I overthrew the enemies of Osiris.' And, finally, he makes reference to that point when the procession actually entered the Temple of Osiris at Abydos: 'I accompanied the god into his house.'

This Mesopotamian cylinder seal from the Akkad period shows deities at the New Year, a time of creation. The deity of the abyss, Ea, strides across the sacred mountain, while the sun god Shamash rises from it.

Similar evidence comes from ancient Mesopotamia and from the ancient Semitic Ugaritic civilization on the coast of Syria. An Assyrian building inscription of Sennacherib (704–681 BC) states that the New Year festival house in the capital city of Assur had bronze door plates on the central entryway which depicted the battle between the god Assur (replacing the Babylonian god Marduk) and Tiamat, from the Babylonian epic of creation, *Enuma Elish*. Sennacherib himself played the role of Assur in the ritual battle, which was part of the dramatic performance of the creation epic at the New Year.

Creation and death were the two grand themes, and it was these that informed the ritual processes of the temples and benefited the relative few who could actually gain access to them.

The Sumerian cylinder inscriptions of King Gudea of Lagash, mentioned above, form the most full account that we have from ancient Mesopotamia, and perhaps from any culture, of the entire process of cosmic temple building. One scholar, H. Sauren, believed that the Gudea texts formed the text of a seven-day 'mystery play', performed each year at the temple dedication feast. He assumed that groups of actors, perhaps extending beyond priestly circles, would have been carefully chosen for each year's enactment.

The centre point of ritual drama in the Maya temple was the ballcourt. Ballcourts were an integral part of the architecture of the sacred plaza, as for example at Tikal, where the most important one was situated between Temple I and the Central Acropolis, and at Copan, where the ballcourt served visually to unify the plaza with the main acropolis. The ballcourt games were based on the myth of the Hero Twins, as recounted in the *Popol Vuh*. The sacred twins were born of the union of a daughter of a Lord of the Underworld with one of the sacrificed brother-pair, the two best human ballplayers. The divine twins represented heavenly bodies, and the ballgames, mostly played out between victorious and vanquished lords with the purpose of supplying blood sacrifice, represented the on-going battle between kings and the Lords of the Underworld. The cosmic battle was waged within the temple complex, on the ballcourt, where kings would actually don the garb of the Hero Twins and engage in combat with opponents dressed as various Lords of the Underworld. The victory of the king would be followed by the public spectacle of blood sacrifice, the blood that was 'the mortar of Maya dynastic life' (Linda Schele).

The theatrical staging of the creation myths and of the mysteries of the afterlife in ancient temples, with initiates playing various roles, was the central ritual process in a society that had been cosmicized by the creation of the temple.

The Gudea inscriptions underline one of the most persistent themes in the ancient creation myths, which is that the purpose and meaning of creation is to be found in the culminating act: the creation of the temple itself. It was only with the founding of the temple that societies were thought to come into existence, since the temple cosmicized and legitimized the society and its kingship. The 'Heavenly Jerusalem' that is brought down to earth at the end of time, as recorded in the Revelation of John, and as is made clear in the Qumran Temple Scroll, is one vast temple. The city has become totally sanctified as a temple, which is the ultimate blessing that a city can experience. The texts also make it clear that if the temples ceased to exist, then the cosmic order on which the society was based, and which gave it its legitimacy, was withdrawn.

The theatrical staging of the creation myths and of the mysteries of the afterlife in ancient temples, with initiates playing various roles, was the central ritual process in a society that had been cosmicized by the creation of the temple. It reinforced the most important religious and psychological information needed for a satisfying life and hope for a glorious afterlife. Most importantly, as Mircea Eliade wrote: 'The profound reason for all these symbols is clear: the temple is the image of the sanctified world. The holiness of the temple sanctifies both the cosmos and cosmic time. Therefore, the temple represents the original state of the world: the pure world that was not worn out by time or sullied by an invasion of the profane.'

A central feature of Monte Albán in Oaxaca, Mexico, was the ballcourt. Games had social importance as the court formed part of the ceremonial plaza.

THE HOUSE OF LIFE

ALL of the great temple traditions have been literate. As soon as writing was invented, it was used to record sacred texts. Some scholars believe that writing was discovered in ancient Sumer and in Egypt under the impetus of ritual, and the concomitant need to record creation myths, rituals and other sacred histories. In any case, as soon as writing was invented in Sumer and Egypt, about the middle of the 4th millennium BC, libraries were built into the great temples to store many different types of texts, including business, diplomatic and sacred. The earliest libraries were temple libraries, and particularly in Egypt this institution is well documented in the form of the *pr 'nkh*, the 'House of Life', which combined, usually within the temple complex, a library, a scriptorium and a general college for the instruction in all the sacred sciences and the professions related to these sciences: medicine, art, architecture, sculpture, astronomy and mathematics.

The earliest libraries were temple libraries … this institution is well documented in the form of the pr 'nkh, *the 'House of Life', which combined, usually within the temple complex, a library, a scriptorium and a general college.*

It was in the Houses of Life that the religious books of ancient Egypt were both written and stored. They were the 'sacred [that is god's] books', 'god's words', 'divine writings'. These were classified as mysteries, and were not to be seen by the uninitiated. One text states, 'It [the House of Life] shall be very hidden and very large. It shall not be known, nor shall it be seen; but the sun shall look upon its mystery. The people who enter into it are the staff of Re and the scribes of the House of Life'.

→ Egyptian text, hieroglyphics, would have been painted or inscribed on the walls of tombs as well as on papyri. This wall painting from the tomb of Pashedu, Thebes, depicts Pashedu praying; behind him are quotes from the *Book of the Dead*.

Spell 146 of the ancient Egyptian *Book of the Dead* instructs on how to enter the mysterious portals of the House of Osiris. In this vignette are five of the twenty-one entrances, each with their doorkeeper.

Another text refers to 'the hymns of worship written by the staff of the House of Life and given to the head teacher of the singers, and the like shall be written in the books of the House of Life'. And, further, 'O all ye priests who penetrate into the words of god and are skilled in writings, ye who are enlightened in the House of Life and have discovered the ways [?] of the gods, who have penetrated into the archives of the Library and can interpret the mysteries of the Emanations of Re [namely, the sacred books], who are skilled in the work of the Ancestors and who open up [?] the heart of what is upon the wall, ye who carve the tombs and who interpret the mysteries ....'

We know that Pharaoh Ramesses IV (1151–1145 BC) spent a considerable amount of time in the House of Life at Abydos researching the 'mysterious forms' of Osiris, and comparing them with all the other gods: 'I have not left unseen any of them all, in order to search out both great and small among the gods and goddesses, and I have found ... the entire Ennead, and all thy forms are more mysterious than theirs.' It is probable that the entire afterlife literature that is so well known from the tombs, coffins and 'books' was composed in the Houses of Life. This included that most famous product of the Egyptian mind, the *Book of the Dead*.

This is not to say that there were not other, more traditional types of libraries attached to the temples, whose purpose was essentially only the storage of books related to the temple. These more traditional temple libraries are to be distinguished from the Houses of Life in that the latter were more far-reaching, comprehensive centres for research, composition, possibly instruction, and storage of books, all relating to the full range of the Egyptian sciences that were devoted to maintaining and perpetuating life. According to one scholar, the House of Life was actually the original temple. In any case, it was the resource from which the priesthoods drew their ritual information and instructions, their own training, the entire range of funerary literature and ritual, insofar as these were employed in the temple cult, and the ritual spells and prayers that were composed for devotees. Gardiner refers to 'magical spells intended for the use of the living' that were composed in the House of Life.

Perhaps no ancient temple fits better the pattern of creation texts used in dramatic ritual being stored in a library near the temple than the Temple of Baal, in the ancient Canaanite city of Ugarit (modern-day Ras Shamra), on the coast of Syria. The city of Ugarit (which flourished between about 1600 and 1200 BC), excavated by French archaeologists since 1939, has yielded some of the most spectacular and important remains of an ancient city and of its cultural heritage that we have.

The Temple of Baal was located on the acropolis of the ancient city, and nearby was a building identified by the excavator as a library or scribal rectory. It was in the ruins of this building that most of the epic and mythic texts in the Ugaritic language (closely related to Biblical Hebrew) were found. The epic of Baal, similar in theme to the Babylonian creation epic *Enuma Elish*, depicts the divine council in heaven, the epic struggle between Baal (the son of the bearded god, El, the Creator of Creatures who lived at the Sources of the Two Waters) and the cosmic waters, personified by Yamm (god of the sea). The highlight of the epic, as also in *Enuma Elish*, is the building of the temples to the victorious god, in this case Baal, a temple of cedar, lapis lazuli, gold and silver, high in the fastness of Mount Zaphon, the cosmic mountain of the North.

The Temple of Baal was located on the acropolis of the ancient city, and nearby was a building identified by the excavator as a library or scribal rectory.

Analogies with *Enuma Elish* (which, as pointed out above, was certainly the text of temple dramas in the Assyrian capital of Assur), the nature of the Ugaritic epics themselves (like the Egyptian mystery plays, they are filled with dramatic dialogue between the divine actors), and our increasing understanding of the role of ritual dramas in ancient Near Eastern temples, plus the find spot of the texts themselves (in the house of a priest, near the Temple of Baal), all point towards the texts forming the basis of temple dramas celebrating the cosmic creation. Additional evidence points toward the Ugaritic epics being performed in the temple at the New Year, at which time there was a celebration of the cosmic creation, divine kingship and the cycles of nature.

→ Stela of the storm god Baal,
found near the Temple of Baal at
Ugarit (modern-day Ras Shamra in
Syria), from the first half of the 2nd
millennium BC. The stone would have
stood in the temple courtyard.

SECRECY

THE temple preserves and transmits the esoteric tradition, the mysteries. Access to the rituals by which these mysteries are transmitted in the temple is restricted, and the knowledge of them is supposed to be kept secret from the uninitiated. Even in modern society, where 'there are no more secrets', and accounts of the initiatic procedures of various temple communities are widely published, such publications still do not give the uninitiated genuine knowledge of the esoteric traditions of the community in question because a ritual is something that must be experienced in order for it to become alive. Reading about it is not enough. Further, in a living ritual tradition there are oral practices at work, 'secrets', which are known within the tradition by priestly functionaries, and which are passed on only in the ceremony itself. Anyone who has actually witnessed a temple initiation, such as I have described above, and has then read one of the books that purports to 'reveal' its innermost secrets will know the difference, and will know how much of the living ritual will have been left out of the book.

Even in modern society, publications still do not give the uninitiated genuine knowledge ... a ritual is something that must be experienced in order for it to become alive.

→ Until the 16th century, Bengali worship of the Hindu goddess Durga, shown here inhabiting a temple in an Indian manuscript painting, c. 1800, was dark, secretive and mysterious. It later developed into a very public affair, with lavish ceremonies encompassing whole communities.

Another Egyptian text dealing with this subject puts us into the milieu of secrecy: a book of magic that was to be composed on the twentieth day of the Nile flood: Thou shalt not divulge it. He who divulges it dies a sudden death and an immediate cutting-off. 'Thou shalt keep very far away from it; by it one lives and dies. It is only to be read by a scribe of the workshop [?] whose name is in the House of Life.' The logic here is very simple but also compelling: if a society possesses the temple ideology, then it will possess mysteries, namely the mysteries of creation, the afterlife, and cosmic matters in general. These mysteries will be dispensed to a select few in the temple through initiation ritual. Initiates will be commanded to keep their knowledge and experiences secret from outsiders.

The Egyptian religious literature is full of this, as for example Spell 114 of the *Book of the Dead* (in Faulkner's translation): 'I know it, for I have been initiated into it by the Sem priest, and I have never spoken nor made repetition to the gods ... I have entered as a Power because of what I know, I have not spoken to men, I have not repeated what was said.' The concluding phrases of Spell 162 of the *Book of the Dead* refers to a secret book: 'This is a book of great secrecy – let no one see it for that would be an abomination. But the one who knows it and keeps it hidden shall continue to exist. The name of this book is "Mistress of the Hidden Temple"'.

Sacred precincts ... can only be entered with great caution, with proper ritual preparations, and with the proper authority. Any other approach could result in disaster.

The reasons for this secrecy, which strikes many in the Western world as bizarre, unnecessary, primitive, undemocratic or even childish, are that what is being done is sacred, holy, something revealed by the gods, not to be trampled upon by the uninitiated or by those who do not understand. There is a strict demarcation between sacred and profane space, although, as I indicated above, any space can be made sacred by an authorized spiritual master within a given tradition, or even by a direct revelation from divinity to an individual at a specific locale (Genesis 28:10–22 – Jacob's dream at Bethel; see p. 46). But once sacred precincts have been demarcated, through having become cosmicized, they can only be entered with great caution, with proper ritual preparations, and with the proper authority. Any other approach could result in disaster: 'And he slew some of the men of Bethshemesh, because they looked into the ark of the Lord' (1 Samuel 6:19).

The aspect of secrecy is reflected in the architecture of the temple. Once the sacred temenos was established and oriented to the heavens according to the sacred geometry, it became off-limits to profane activity and profane people. Ancient Norse sanctuaries, known as *ve*, were separated off from profane activity by a *vebond*, a string or rope, or by a fence, just as shrines in the Greek world were encircled by a red band, or as the Agora in Athens was surrounded and set off by a special kind of rope, the *perischoinisma*. The very fact that temples were considered to be mountains, in touch with the heavenly spheres, meant that they were sited on artificial or natural hilltops, which gradually became higher and higher over hundreds of years of continued building activity; their very height, combined with ramparts, could make them inaccessible to the common people.

Temple I at Tikal, Guatemala, sits atop a solid stone pyramid. Accessible only to the priests and the chosen few, who had to climb the precipitous staircase (often when they were in costume and laden with offerings), the interior of the building was a series of small rooms where hushed ceremonies would have been performed.

> The numinous,
> the sacred,
> possess great
> power, which,
> if desecrated,
> can unleash
> considerable
> destructive
> force.

The mandala-like labyrinth on the floor of Chartres cathedral, France.

The most venerable symbol of the inaccessibility of the sacred temple precincts to profane activity, as well as the symbol of the difficulty of approach for the pilgrim, is the labyrinth. The tomb-temples of ancient Egypt, most famously the original Labyrinth, that of Amenemhet III (Twelfth Dynasty), described by Pliny, were constructed in a maze-like fashion, analogous to the mandala. The construction, copied by Daedalus in building the Labyrinth of King Minos on Crete, was intended to create a difficult pathway into the centre for the initiate, and to protect the sacred mysteries from outsiders. Furthermore, since one of the central purposes of the sacred dramas was the reenactment of the death and resurrection of the god, the labyrinth played the role of stage, in which the sacred circular ritual dances were performed, and the god was protected from his [ritual] enemies. The earliest labyrinths that we know are the tortuous pathways into the depths of the Upper Paleolithic caves of France and Spain. Labyrinths were constructed into the floors of Gothic cathedrals, most famously at Chartres, where the mosaic maze was laid into the floor at the crossing of the nave with the chancel, on line with the main altar, symbolically protecting the Holy of Holies from direct access, or making that access difficult, as access to the centre must always be.

The numinous, the sacred, possess great power (called in the Biblical scriptures 'the wrath of God'), which, if desecrated, can unleash considerable destructive force. Obviously, people are not killed today for transgressing the strict rules of secrecy that are associated with temple ritual. Such strictures are now, and probably always were, as a general rule, metaphors for the loss of the spiritual power attained in the initiation by the individual who revealed the secrets. As Lohengrin says in the 'recital of the Grail' section in Wagner's opera, 'And its [the Grail's] power is sacred as long as it remains unknown to all.' In many cases, the secrets are culturally or ethnically based, and provide a stronghold of inner, communal strength against the inroads of outsiders whose influence would contribute to the destruction of social cohesion that is fostered by the rituals.

The mosaic maze at medieval Chartres cathedral, France, is walked by pilgrims today. The labyrinth was initially created to symbolically restrict access to the Holy of Holies.

The granite shrine in the inner sanctum of the Temple of Horus at Edfu, Egypt, was the holiest part of the temple. The 4-metre-high (13-ft) block is the oldest part of the temple and likely contained a wooden cult image of Horus.

Since the ultimate role and meaning of temple ritual is spiritual, the only harm that can result from betraying the secrets is to the inner spiritual life of the initiate himself.

An inscription on one of the doors of the Temple of Edfu states: 'Do not reveal what you have seen in the mysteries of the temple.' The Edfu texts give us insight into the nature of restrictions on entry into the temple. The vast majority of Egyptians were forbidden entry. The south gate of the temenos of the Edfu temple bore inscriptions which stated: 'It is the standing place of those who have and those who have not in order to pray for life from the Lord of Life ... The place for hearing the petitions of all petitioners in order to judge Truth from Falsehood. It is the great place for championing the poor in order to rescue them from the strong ... The place outside which offerings are made at all times consisting of all the produce of the servants.' In other words, this wall was the furthest extent of entryway into the temple precincts that the common people were allowed. And it was at this place that they offered up their petitions.

Similar restrictions have been common in many temple societies, although, in the case of Tibetan Buddhism, members of the general public, including non-Buddhists, are now invited to attend the most sacred, and, until recent years the most secret, temple (mandala) rituals. As His Holiness the Dalai Lama has said, the contents of the Tibetan rituals are now 'an open secret', and he wishes to ensure that correct and accurate information concerning these rituals be made available.

Since the ultimate role and meaning of temple ritual is spiritual, the only harm that can result from betraying the secrets is to the inner spiritual life of the initiate himself. Those who, in a modern, open society, observe a ritual with some degree of curiosity, without personal involvement or understanding, can hardly be harmed, and indeed will doubtless be blessed, by the spiritual power of what they witness. One of the greatest problems of secret rituals, now as in antiquity, is that some of the uninitiated spread grossly false rumours about the rituals, based on partial or distorted information. This is especially true of some of the Greek descriptions of Egyptian ritual (which most of the Greek writers were not able to witness first hand), and it is also true of those 20th-century accounts of Tibetan ritual which emphasize the supposed sexual nature of the rituals.

MOST of the great temple-building societies have believed in the power of the temple, that dynamo of life and of power that is built over the primordial mound of creation, to restore life after death. Temple precincts have often become centres for burial, and the rituals of creation include accounts of deities such as Osiris in ancient Egypt, who was restored from death to his role as the permanent god of the underworld and symbol of the renewal of life after death. The earthly temple, a replica of a temple in heaven, gives human beings a glimpse of the eternal life that is lived in the heavens. Humans were separated from the gods at the time of creation, when they were expelled from the paradise that they shared with them. The temple, with its artificial or natural, paradise, its tree and waters of life, is the centre point of existence on earth, the place where death can be overcome.

The tomb was the ultimate inner sanctum, where the mysteries of creation, death and resurrection culminated.

→ Mastaba tombs, like this restored entrance at Saqqara, Egypt, were made up of an underground burial site with a rectangular superstructure built from stone or mud-brick above the subterranean chamber.

In Egypt, tombs were essentially temples in that they were cosmically oriented, involved the deceased in the underworld funerary ritual, and were places of resurrection. Tombs were places of primordial power, and in fact, the inner burial chamber of the Archaic Period mastaba royal tombs at Saqqara was covered with a mound of earth, reminiscent of the mound tombs of the same period from Abydos. This mound represented the primordial mound of creation, just like the inner sanctum of Egyptian temples. The tomb was the ultimate inner sanctum, where the mysteries of creation, death and resurrection culminated.

The tomb and temple could be united on the same spot, as in the funerary temple of Mentuhotep (2060–2010 BC) at Deir el-Bahri. The king's tomb was built into the cliff at Deir el-Bahri, at the western end of the temple complex, and in front of the main shrine, where his funerary rituals could be performed.

The mortuary temples of Mentuhotep and Hatshepsut built into the rock face at Deir el-Bahri, Egypt.

Egyptian sarcophagi were carved with inscriptions to the gods to help the deceased in the underworld.

The strongest connection that can be made in ancient Egypt between the temple and burial is based on the prehistoric cult shrine of Upper Egypt, the *Pr-wr*, or Great House, of the early capital of Hierakonpolis. This earliest shrine was incorporated into the funerary architecture of the New Kingdom, where coffins were built in its shape, and in the Temple of Sethos I at Abydos, where the innermost chapels in honour of Osiris, Horus, Isis, Ptah, Amen-Re and Re-Harakhte were fashioned after the design of the primitive Upper Egyptian temple. Coffins also typically show the Egyptian sky goddess Nut, painted onto the inner ceiling, which adds the cosmic dimension to this 'sacred place'. The Egyptian inscriptions contain the phrase, 'Nut is the coffin.' Thus the tomb was assimilated to the temple, and both became places of resurrection.

The funerary rites of the ancient temples were associated with the underworld, where the power to overcome death, in the form of the sacred tree and waters, originated (*see also p. 75*). The Eninnu Temple in ancient Lagash had, according to the inscriptions of Gudea, a chapel called 'the house in which one brings offerings for the dead', said to be 'something pure, purified by *Abzu*'.

Archaeological excavations in many parts of the world have noted the tendency for a sacred precinct to draw large numbers of burials to it. A classic example of this is a series of prehistoric temples at the site of Tepe Gawra, in northern Iraq. According to the excavator, Level XI in particular 'attracted considerable numbers of burials to its precincts'. This same phenomenon has also become clear through excavations around the Temple Mount in Jerusalem, where famous Hellenistic Period royal burials are well known in the Valley of Kidron, flanking the Temple Mount on the east, and now, in more recent excavations, royal burial places of the Kings of Judah may have been discovered on the northern edge of the Temple Mount.

The Delphic Oracle, the ancient Greek centre of the world, was situated at the sanctuary of Apollo on the lower slopes of Mount Parnassus.

Likewise the temples at Angkor, in Cambodia, served as 'royal mausolea', which received the remains or ashes of deceased kings. The great French scholar, Paul Mus, relates the Buddhist stupa to the role of the temple as a place of burial: 'We have before us a sepulchre which is also in fact, a temple. It is a sanctuary tomb ... The tomb becomes not so much a shelter for the dead, as a kind of new architectural body, substituted for the mortal remains of a deceased "cosmic man" where his magic soul will live on and prolong his existence.'

The centre of the 6th-century BC libation phiale, *above left*, represents the Omphalos, and the image on the kylix (drinking cup) from c. 440 BC, *above right*, shows the Oracle at Delphi – a woman with a special link to the gods – consulting the primordial waters.

The Omphalos Stone at the Oracle at Delphi took the shape of the tumulus, the burial mound, which was analogous with the original mound of creation. It was actually thought to be the grave of the dismembered Dionysus. Through the Omphalos (the navel or centre of the earth) one gained access to the underworld and its mysteries. Life and death combine at this place and in this image, the one arising from the other. A characteristic ancient Greek libation basin, the phiale, was frequently made in the shape of a shallow, slightly curved saucer, with a hump in the centre. These were known as 'omphalos basins'. The omphalos rises out of the water that stands in the dish as an offering, just as in Egypt and ancient Israel the mound of creation was seen as arising up out of the primordial waters of creation. This is the 'living water', the water that gives life to the deceased for whom it is offered.

The role of the sacred mound in overcoming death is also tied in very closely with the ancestors, because, by definition, the dead, having been reunited with the sources of life in the underworld, are numinous, and begin at their death to exert these powers on behalf of the living. Throughout Scandinavia the sacred Althing, the place of law-giving, judgment and other royal acts, was located on a mountain, where, previously, the burials of ancestors had been sited. Examples have been preserved from pre-Christian times in Sweden where the king's throne, along with a monument honouring an ancestor, were located together at the top of a sacred mountain.

The site of Palenque in the Usumacinta river basin in Mexico gives us an extraordinary example of the burial of a royal personage, centred deep within the heart of a pyramid temple. The Temple of the Inscriptions, dated to the Maya Classic Period (about the 7th century AD) seems to have been built to house the tomb of the exceptional individual buried there (p. 35). The access to the tomb was constructed through a floor in the main temple, which was then blocked and hidden through elaborate masonry slabs and rubble. An interior stairway, roofed with corbel vaulting, led down to the burial vault, which was constructed 1.8 metres (6 ft) below ground level, as a cave deep within the earth. There, the excavator found a monolithic sarcophagus in the shape of a uterus. The skeleton (of the Maya king Pacal) was covered with jade. The sides of the sarcophagus were covered with bas-reliefs depicting ten of Pacal's ancestors.

A divine Tree of Life rises up out of the depths of the cave that the temple shelters, and unites the three world regions. It was along the trunk of this tree that the deceased and the gods travelled from world level to level.

Each ancestor is shown rising through the cracked earth with a different species of fruit tree. The lid of the sarcophagus contained an elaborate carving of the Maya Tree of Life. The Tree of Life in Maya mythology, the ceiba tree, united the three cosmic regions, and provided food and drink at its roots. Here it rises out of the cave at the centre of the earth, the Maya hell Xibalba, as the *axis mundi*. A celestial bird sat perched at its top, while a serpent wrapped itself around it at the Middleworld, or earthly level. As the trunk of the tree sank into the underworld, it was swallowed by the open maw of death. A stone tube connected the burial chamber, along the staircase, with the temple above, which provided access to the world of the living for the ancestors, who would communicate through the Vision Serpent, the deity that provided interaction between the two worlds.

→ A Maya sarcophagus lid, AD 683, recording the burial deep inside the Temple of the Inscriptions, Palenque, of King Pacal.

An image of the sun on its passage from east to west, in between the two realms of life and death, was carved at the top of the sarcophagus lid, since the descent of the sun into Xibalba would take the king with it, while its rising would assure the king victory over death. The Temple of the Inscriptions was constructed of nine distinct building levels, corresponding to the nine levels of the Maya underworld.

Here we have in the Mesoamerican realm the same combination of temple-centred influences that we have seen in several other cultures: 1) a temple on top of a pyramid that has been built with astronomical orientation suggesting the idea of bringing a heavenly model down to earth, creating the sacred mountain; 2) a burial deep beneath the pyramid, suggesting the idea that life comes originally out of the earth, and that death is overcome by returning the body to the depths of the temple, to the First Mother, where the primeval power of original creation is most powerful, and where the deceased will rise, like the sun, from the underworld. A divine Tree of Life rises up out of the depths of the cave that the temple shelters, and unites the three world regions. It was along the trunk of this tree that the deceased and the gods travelled from world level to level.

The connection between the temple, death, burial and the afterlife finds remarkable expression in the Book of Isaiah, chapter 25, verses 6–8. The context here is the covenant feast which brings all people together after the New Year festival at the temple, where chaos has been overcome and the people can rejoice together ('On this mountain the Lord of Hosts will make for all peoples a feast'). Since the majority of people could not actually witness the ceremony in the temple ('On this mountain'), it was through the covenant-making feast that concluded the temple ceremonies that they become partakers of the blessings of the temple renewal and of the cosmic renewal of society. In this case, however, the setting is the messianic meal which the Messiah will share with all people in the messianic temple at the end of time, when the ultimate enemy of cosmic unity, death, will have been overcome: 'He will swallow up death forever, the Lord God will wipe away tears from all faces ...' (25:8).

The idea of the sacred mountain persists even when religions change. This Christian calvary is built on the site of an Aztec temple at Cholula, Mexico. The lithograph is by José Luciano Castañeda and is thought to be from around 1805.

Within the Christian tradition, this passage finds its fulfilment in the Revelation of John, where the Messiah sits 'within his temple' (the heavenly temple that has descended onto the earth, like the messianic temple of the Qumran community, that has taken up the entire city of Jerusalem) and the throngs of people who have experienced tribulation 'he will guide ... to springs of living water; and God will wipe away every tear from their eyes' (Revelation 7:15–17). Thus we come back full circle to the point where this essay began: the mountain as temple, with its life-giving waters bubbling up from sources deep within the primordial abyss, possessing the power to overcome death. The temple, perhaps the most powerful and all-encompassing expression of the sacred in human society, brings together in its architecture, its symbolism and its ritual the most central features of the religious life of humankind.

THE TEMPLE'S MANY FORMS

Throughout history, the urge to build temples has generated an instinctive impulse towards abstract geometry, though all its forms can be seen as in some sense originating in the primordial mound. The influence can be seen in temples all around the world, including the ziggurat at Ur (*below left*); the Shore Temple at Mamallapuram, India (*bottom left*); the temple of Tikal, Guatemala (*below right*); and the Al Azhar Mosque, Cairo (*opposite, bottom left*).

In the West, temples and churches have assumed a variety of forms, but all are recognizably religious: for example, the temple of Hephaistos at Athens (*opposite, below right*) and the stave church at Borgund, Norway (*opposite, above left*). A series of models (*opposite, above right*) reduces the forms of sacred buildings to their geometrical essentials. The Egyptian pyramid, Islamic mosque, Christian church and Greek temple can all be generated from half a dozen simple elements.

Ziggurat at Ur. Reconstructed by the archaeologist Leonard Woolley.

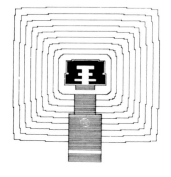

The 8th-century Shore Temple at Mamallapuram, India.

Section through the Maya temple of Tikal, Guatemala.

12th-century Norwegian stave church
at Borgund.

A selection of temple models made by German Expressionist
designer Hermann Finsterlin in 1922.

Al Azhar Mosque, Cairo. A Fatimid mosque,
built in 970–72.

The best preserved of all Greek temples: the temple of
Hephaistos at Athens from the mid-5th century BC.

THE PRIMORDIAL MOUND

The first holy sites were probably mountains. Today many of the most outstanding shrines involve the upward path and the deity who dwells in the high places. Temples may be built on the top of mounds, or artificial mounds may be constructed for them, or they may suggest the form of hills in their architecture. The mound also had an association with death, as shown by the burial mounds of Swedish kings in Uppsala (*below left*). The Omphalos Stone at Delphi was based on the shape of a burial mound; it was through this 'navel of the world' that an individual could gain access to the underworld.

The 'Royal Mounds' of Uppsala, Sweden; burial cairns of ancient kings from the 5th or 6th century.

An Aztec throne, AD 1507, made in the form of a temple built on top of a ziggurat.

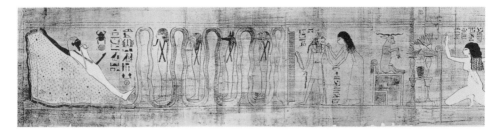

Ithyphallic image of Osiris, god of the afterlife, reclining on a primordial mound. Drawing on Egyptian papyrus.

What the Greek Omphalos Stone at Delphi might have looked like.

The Great Stupa at Sanchi, India, built in the 1st century AD.

An omphalos stone.

Small votive stupa from the 9th century. Made in Nalanda, India.

THE PATH INWARD

Temples use the image of the cave to express the numinous power of the inner journey and the still profundity of the Holy of Holies. In the Hindu temple of Phnom Kulen, the sacred lingam stands in a man-made cavern (*opposite, above left*). At Karli, near Bombay (*opposite, above right*), the temple is a real cave, and the architecture and sculpture, including the elephants, the stupa at the end and the ceremonial umbrella over it, are all miraculously carved from the living rock. The Dome of the Rock in Jerusalem traditionally preserves the threshing floor above which King Solomon built his Temple (*opposite, below left*). This was the spot from which Mohammed was taken up into Heaven, and which became the Holy of Holies.

Exterior of the Mai-chi-shan cave temples in China. Built during the Northern Wei Dynasty (AD 386–534).

Indian sculpture of Indra's visit to the Buddha. Relief from Mathura in Uttar Pradesh, India.

Drawing of the Hindu cave temple at Karli, near Bombay, by Thomas and William Daniell, c. 1793.

Temple at Phnom Kulen, Cambodia, with an early 9th-century stone lingam placed in the centre of the subterranean room.

The threshing floor inside the Dome of the Rock, Jerusalem. The construction of the holy site began in AD 691.

Mexican drawing of a Toltec initiate passing through channels to be born.

THE HEAVENLY PRESENCE

The purpose of the elaborate rituals that accompanied the choice of site, the laying out of the temple precinct and its consecration was to secure the god's approval, something which can be represented in art in a variety of symbolic ways. Mohammed (*below left*) saw an angel bringing down the sacred precinct from Heaven, and by a similar convention St Augustine is shown inspired by a vision of the City of God as he writes his famous book (*opposite, above left*).

Unseen gods inhabit the temples that men build for them, and their presence can only be shown conventionally. In a Japanese painting from Kumano (*opposite, centre right*), the deities to whom the various shrines are dedicated appear above them in circular panels like portraits. In this painting of Wutai Shan (*opposite, top right*), China, the region is filled with temples, monasteries and sacred caves. Here the gods' presence is signalled by their appearance in a cloud that looks like smoke.

In Christianity, the use of images to portray divine beings has been controversial. Iconoclastic movements at various periods have insisted that God cannot be represented in bodily form. More normally, images have been used to aid and embody the spiritual experiences of the worshippers. Some icons (*opposite, below left*) explicitly place Jesus, the Virgin and saints in the chapels of a church.

Mohammed witnessing an angel bringing down the sacred precinct from heaven.

A tabernacle, the earliest prototype for the temple in Jerusalem, with a cloud hovering above it.

Panorama of the holy site of Wutai Shan, China.

Letter from an illuminated manuscript showing St Augustine inspired by a vision as he writes his book *The City of God*. Italian painting from the 15th century.

Late 14th-century Shinto mandala painting from Kumano, Japan.

Russian icon from the 16th century showing the figure of Christ inside a church.

15th-century relief of the story of Cain and Abel by Italian Renaissance sculptor Lorenzo Ghiberti. God is shown in the clouds above the mountain.

SACRED GEOMETRY

It was vitally important to choose a site pleasing to the gods, correctly aligned with the cardinal directions, and constructed with the appropriate ritual observances. In Egypt the pharaoh himself broke the soil with a hoe (*below left*). The tomb of Senmut at Deir el-Bahri has a ceiling (*opposite, top left*) carved with astronomical calculations which had to be mastered in laying out a sacred building. In Islam, every mosque has to be aligned so that the worshippers face Mecca (*opposite, bottom right*).

The science of surveying probably arose through the need to set out sacred buildings correctly. These feats of precise applied geometry are among the most astonishing achievements of the ancient world. The great temple-complexes of the Aztecs, such as Teotihuacán (*opposite, bottom left*), involved huge structures, all aligned on axes that could stretch for many miles. Equally impressive was the building of Angkor Wat, a vast mandala in stone, a unique combination of mysticism and engineering (*opposite, above right*). The temple entrances all face west, so that the rising sun is aligned with the topmost tower at the equinoxes and the solstices. On a much smaller scale, a statuette of King Gudea holds in his lap the plan revealed to him during the night in a temple, which is as clear and functional as any modern blueprint (*below right; opposite, centre left*).

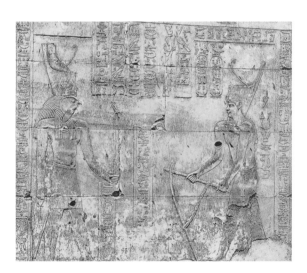

Relief from the Temple of Horus at Edfu. Built in the Ptolemaic Period.

Statuette of King Gudea, ruler of Sumerian Lagash in the 3rd millennium BC. His temple plan is etched onto the lap of the figurine (*opposite, centre left*).

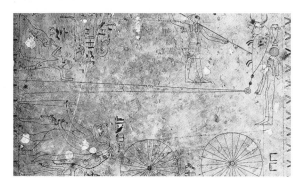

Astronomical calculations from the ceiling of the tomb
of Senmut at Deir el-Bahri. Decoration from *c.* 1500 BC.

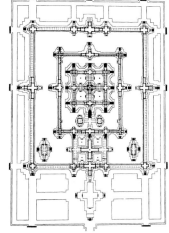

Detail of the plan
for King Gudea's
temple engraved on
the lap of a statuette
(*opposite, right*).

Ground plan of the Angkor Wat site. The plan is
itself a mandala, and many of the towers relate
to astronomical calculations.

16th-century map of the Muslim world. The
Kaabah is in the centre with lines radiating
from it; it is on these lines that various mosques
around the Mediterranean are placed.

Teotihuacán's massive ziggurats, ballcourts, processional paths
and palaces.

MANDALAS

A mandala is a geometrical pattern embodying a spiritual truth. Brought to its greatest pitch of sophistication by Tibetan Buddhists, its essentials can nevertheless be found in the religious art of far distant times and places. Mandalas can be drawn out on the ground, and the plan of Borobudur (*opposite, above left*) – something which could never be seen except with the mind's eye – has all the characteristics of one. Uniting the square and the circle, it can work as the focus for meditation like the classic Tibetan example, a Kalachakra mandala (*opposite, below left*). The back of a Chinese mirror, with its circle, square and symbolic 'animals of the four quarters', is also a recognizable form of mandala (*below left*). Other religions have used pattern, symbolism and geometry in ways that similarly represent mystical experience in graphic form. Some are still enigmatic, such as the patterned Norse stone from Sanda, in Sweden (*opposite, right*). Others are luminously clear, like the vault over the chancel of San Vitale at Ravenna (*below right*): in the centre is the Lamb of God, supported by four angels and in the corners are peacocks, symbols of eternal life.

A mandala on the reverse of a bronze Chinese mirror from the Han Dynasty (206 BC–AD 220).

The vault over the 6th-century chancel of San Vitale at Ravenna, Italy.

Ground plan of the temple of Borobudur in Java, Indonesia.

Norse stone from Sweden, *c.* AD 500.

Tibetan Kalachakra mandala painting from the 16th century.

BOROBUDUR

The great Buddhist shrine of Borobudur, in Java, is the most complex but also the most lucidly organized temple in the world. Its six lower levels are square, the four upper ones circular. Each level contains Buddha figures gazing out across the countryside in the cardinal directions. At the top is a series of stupas with square or diamond-shaped openings, originally each housing a figure of the Buddha. As pilgrims walked round each level they passed long sculptured friezes describing the lives of the Buddha on earth, so that there was both a circumambulatory and an upward movement, symbolizing the process of enlightenment through initiation.

Stone frieze at Borobudur. In total, the reliefs extend over 6 km (3.7 miles).

Stone sculpture of a Dhyani Buddha.

Buddha figure in an arch. Built between AD 750 and AD 842.

The lattice-work stone 'bells' each enclose a Buddha. There are seventy-two
of these stupas at the shrine, of which the biggest is at the summit.

THE TEMPLE OF THE LORD

For the Jews there is only one Temple, that first built in Jerusalem by King Solomon, rebuilt by Herod the Great and destroyed by the Romans in AD 70. Almost no trace of it remains, but throughout the Middle Ages Jerusalem was seen as the centre of the world. A schematic map (*opposite, top right*) shows Europe, Asia and Africa like three petals springing from it. The first Temple was the resting place of the Ark of the Covenant (*below right*). On the basis of written descriptions in the Bible, many extraordinary attempts have been made to reconstruct how the Temple appeared (*opposite, bottom left*). Today part of its substructure is sacred to the Jews.

After the Muslims conquered Jerusalem they built the mosque known as the Dome of the Rock (*below left*) over what was thought to have been the Holy of Holies of Solomon's Temple. It was a spot venerated by Islam as well as by Judaism and Christianity. When the Crusaders in turn became masters of Jerusalem, they transformed the mosque into a church and (with their limited knowledge of architectural history) took it to be the Temple itself. It appears prominently in such illustrated books as Hartmann Schedel's *Nuremberg Chronicle* of 1493 (*opposite, above left*), labelled 'Templum Salomonis', and in the backgrounds of several Renaissance paintings. It even influenced Jewish iconography of the Temple.

The Dome of the Rock, a holy site for Jews, Christians and Muslims.

6th-century mosaic of the Ark of the Covenant, from Kwuzat Hefzibah, Israel.

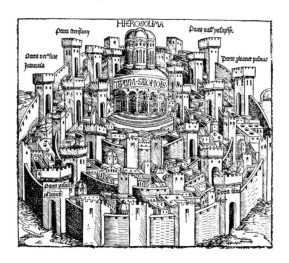

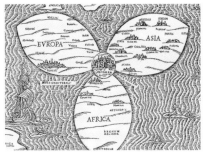

Schematic world map that puts Jerusalem
at the centre of the world. Drawn in 1581
by Heinrich Bunting.

Illustration of the Dome of the Rock from the *Nuremberg Chronicle*
by Hartmann Schedel, 1493.

Reconstruction of the first Temple, Jerusalem,
by Bernard Lamy. Drawn in 1720.

Worshippers in 1899 at the Wailing Wall in Jerusalem,
a site for Jewish prayer and pilgrimage then as today.

THE WAY OF THE PILGRIM

Pilgrimage is a journey to the divine source. It usually incorporates one or several of the features that we have found to be associated with temples: the ascent of a sacred mountain or the ritual of circumambulation. Islam has made the pilgrimage to Mecca (*opposite, top*) one of the cornerstones of the faith. Every Muslim is bound, once in his lifetime, to make the journey and circumambulate the Kaabah according to the prescribed ritual. When he returns his house door is marked by a sign to show that he has accomplished the pilgrimage (*below right*). In Buddhism, too, pilgrimage is an act of high merit. A pictorial map (*opposite, centre*) of the route to Mount Kailash shows eight of the monasteries along the way, with the holy mountain itself – white and conical – towards the left. The labyrinth is a symbolic pilgrimage and is found in many sacred contexts, including the Greek precinct of Epidaurus (*opposite, bottom*). Something of the alert and strenuous atmosphere of the past is recaptured in the Irish pilgrimage to Croagh Patrick, with its long line of men and women trudging uphill carrying staves (*below left*).

Irish pilgrims on the journey to Croagh Patrick, County Mayo.

Markings on a doorway show that the occupant has made a pilgrimage to Mecca.

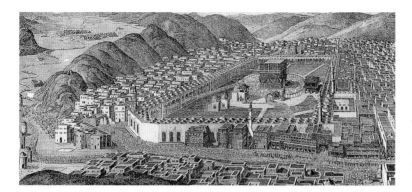

The Kaabah in Mecca. Section from an 18th-century engraving.

Pictoral map of the long path to Mount Kailash in the Himalayas.

Stone labyrinth in Epidaurus, an ancient Greek centre of healing.

THE TREE OF LIFE

Trees are potent symbols of cosmic unity, their roots reaching into the underworld, their branches to heaven. The Judaic myth of the Tree of Knowledge and the Fall of Man is prefigured in Babylonian cylinder seals (*opposite, above right*) showing two figures seated by a sacred tree with a serpent behind the one on the left. The Buddha attained enlightenment under a tree; a relief at Sanchi (*opposite, top left*) features the adoration of the throne and the tree. In Mexico, the Mixtec people were believed to have been born from a womb-tree (*opposite, below right*). But it was in Norse mythology that the tree attained its greatest prominence: the gigantic world-tree Yggdrassil (*below right*) supported the cosmos, with sacred springs at its foot, a serpent at its roots and an eagle in its branches. A single column with a foliate capital can be a symbolic tree – as with that erected by Ashoka at Karli (*below centre*) and the Qutb Minar at Delhi (*below left*). Even in modern Christianity the association of trees with holiness lives on, as in this Thorncrown Chapel at Eureka Springs, Arkansas, in the United States of America (*opposite, below left*).

The Qutb Minar at Delhi, India. Early 13th century.

Column of Ashoka at Karli, India. Drawn by Thomas and William Daniel, *c.* 1792–95.

Icelandic manuscript illustration of Yggdrassil, *c.* 1680.

A late Akkadian cylinder seal with a tree and snake in the centre. Made around 2200 to 2100 BC.

Relief showing the adoration of the throne and the tree, from Sanchi, India.

Mixtec people emerging from a womb-tree. Image from the *Codex Vindobonensis Mexicanus I*.

Chapel built in Arkansas, USA, by E. Fay Jones in 1980.

THE LIVING WATER

From beneath the primordial mound sprang the rivers of paradise – recognition by early agricultural peoples of their dependence upon water for life. Sacred pools figure prominently in the religious rituals of the Aztecs and the Egyptians (*opposite, above right*). At Angkor Wat, the imagery of water and of the churning of the Sea of Milk is part of the cosmic myth (*opposite, below right*). Ancient Mesopotamia, born of the Tigris and the Euphrates, represented the primeval waters as stylized patterns on the façade of the 14th-century BC temple of Karaindash (*below right*). Biblical imagery of the four rivers flowing from paradise (*opposite, below left*), was given added mystical significance in apocalyptic vision (*below left*), where the waters flowing from beneath the throne of God represent the salvation that flows from Christ's sacrifice.

Water stands for salvation in this Flemish painting, c. 1400.

Stone façade of the temple of Karaindash at Uruk (modern-day Iraq). The sculpted brickwork is from the 14th century BC.

The sacred lake at Karnak, Egypt. Located in a large temple complex, the rectangular lake was built by Thutmose III.

A Chinese stupa rises out of the water. The water surrounding stone evokes tranquility charged with divine force.

Relief from Angkor Wat, Cambodia. Four-armed Vishnu is depicted in water, the Sea of Milk, surrounded by asuras and devas.

The four rivers flowing from paradise. Byzantine manuscript of the 12th-century Homilies of Jacob of Kokkinobaphos.

THE TEMPLE AT WORK

Ritual is the technique or process through which the temple functions as a means of communication with the other world. Without the temple, it has been said, ritual is 'a map without territory'. Many of the rituals practised in temples were secret and have been irrecoverably lost. We do not know what took place in them with certainty. A sculptured vase from Uruk (*opposite, right*) seems to show a procession of priests bearing offerings to a goddess, while a painting from Khorsabad (*opposite, above left*) represents King Sargon before a god. The Greek Eleusinian mysteries (*opposite, below left*) are partially known from literary sources, though again some parts were kept secret. Some rituals took the form of dramatic performances which might prefigure the joys of paradise. Celestial beauties in the frieze of the Jain temple at Satnarjaya Hill, near Bombay, dance to the sounds of celestial male musicians (*bottom*). Egyptian ritual is also adequately documented on ancient papyri and such pictures gave later artists the clues to depict realistically the full panoply of an Egyptian rite amid the huge columns of Dendera (*below*).

Rites being
performed at
Dendera, Egypt.

Jain frieze from a temple near Satnarjaya Hill, Bombay.

King Sargon faces a god. Image from
Khorsabad (modern-day Iraq).

Gifts being presented to the gods.
Alabaster vase from Uruk, c. 3000 BC.

4th-century BC red-figure painting of secret rituals being
performed at Eleusis in ancient Greece.

LIFE AFTER DEATH

Temples were the dwellings of powers who could overcome death, and were therefore favoured places in which to await resurrection to eternal life. Temples contained tombs and tombs were miniature temples. The so-called Tomb of Absalom (*below left*), just outside Jerusalem, is a Hellenistic structure carved out of the rock, traditionally identified as the burial place of David's son. Burial stones from Lärbro, Sweden (*opposite, above*) and Mexico (*below right*) depict the soul's journey after death. Prominent on the Norse stone is the ship which carried the dead man's spirit to the other world. The Maya sarcophagus lid records the burial of King Pacal deep inside the temple at Palenque. Far older, and most enigmatic of all, is the so-called 'Shaft of the Dead Man' in the prehistoric caves of Lascaux in France. It is possible that these caves were both temples and burial places (*opposite, below*).

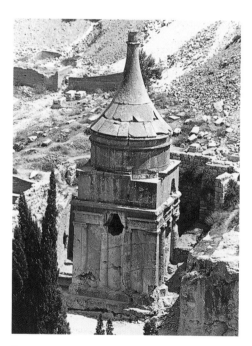

The Tomb of Absalom in the Kidron Valley near Jerusalem.

Rubbing of a Maya sarcophagus lid from AD 683. Found at Palenque, Mexico (*pp. 94–95*).

9th-century Norse picture-stone from Lärbro in Gotland, Sweden.

Cave painting of a human figure next to a bison, at Lascaux, France.

FURTHER READING

BENSON, ELIZABETH P. (ed.), *Mesoamerican Sites and World-Views*, Washington D.C., 1981

BERGQUIST, BIRGITTA, *The Archaic Greek Temenos: A Study of Structure and Function*, Lund, 1967

COEDES, GEORGE, *Angkor: An Introduction*, Singapore, 1963

CORBIN, HENRY, *Temple and Contemplation*, London, 1986

DAVID, ROSALIE, *A Guide to Religious Ritual at Abydos*, Warminster, 1981

DAVIS, RICHARD H., *Ritual in an Oscillating Universe: Worshipping Siva in Medieval India*, Princeton, 1991

DE VRIES, JAN, *Altgermanische Religionsgeschichte*, 2 vols, Berlin, 1956–57 (2nd edn)

ELIADE, MIRCEA, 'The Prestige of the Cosmogonic Myth', *Diogenes 23* (1958), pp. 1–13

ELLIS DAVIDSON, H. R., *Myths and Symbols in Pagan Europe*, Syracuse, 1988

FAULKNER, R. O., *The Ancient Egyptian Book of the Dead*, Austin, 1985

FINNESTAD, RAGNHILD BJERRE, *Image of the World and Symbol of the Creator: On the Cosmological and Iconographical Values of the Temple of Edfu*, Wiesbaden, 1985

GARDINER, ALAN H., 'The House of Life', *Journal of Egyptian Archaeology*, 24 (1938), pp. 157–79

GIEDION, S., *The Beginnings of Architecture* (Bollingen Series, XXXV, 6, II), Princeton, 1964

———, *The Beginnings of Art* (Bollingen Series, XXXV, 6,I), New York, 1962

GOMEZ, LUIS O. and HIRAM W. WOODWARD JR. (eds) *Barabudur, History and Significance of a Buddhist Monument*, Berkeley, 1981

HARRISON, JANE, *Prolegomena to the Study of Greek Religion*, New York, 1959

HOLLANDER, LEE M. (trans.), *The Poetic Edda*, Austin, 1986

HOPKINS, JEFFREY, *Kalachakra Tantra Rite of Initiation*, London, 1985

KRAMRISCH, STELLA, *The Hindu Temple*, 2 vols, Delhi, 1976

LAWLOR, ROBERT, *Sacred Geometry: Philosophy and Practice*, London and New York, 1982

LUNDQUIST, JOHN M., 'The Legitimizing Role of the Temple in the Origin of the State', *Society of Biblical Literature 1982 Seminar Papers*, ed. Kent Harold Richards, Chico, Calif., 1982, pp. 271–96

———, 'What is a Temple? A Preliminary Typology', *The Quest for the Kingdom of God: Studies in Honor of George E. Mendenhall*, ed. H. B. Huffmon, F. A. Spina and A. R. W. Green, Winona Lake, Ind., 1983, pp. 206–19

———, *Studies on the Temple in the Ancient Near East*, University of Michigan PhD Dissertation, Ann Arbor, 1983

———, 'The Common Temple Ideology of the Ancient Near East', *The Temple in Antiquity*, ed. Truman G. Madsen, Provo, Utah, 1984, pp. 53–76

———, 'Temple, Covenant and Law in the Ancient Near East and in the Hebrew Bible', *Israel's Apostasy and Restoration: Essays in Honor of Roland K. Harrison*, ed. Avraham Gileadi, Grand Rapids, Mich., 1988, pp. 293–305

———, 'C. G. Jung and the Temple: Symbols of Wholeness', *C. G. Jung and the Humanities: Toward a Hermeneutics of Culture*, ed. Karin Barnaby and Pellegrino D'Acierno, Princeton, 1990, pp. 113–23

———, *The Temple of Jerusalem: Past, Present, and Future*, Westport, 2007

MACADAMS, CYNTHIA, HUNBATZ MEN and CHARLES BENSINGER, *Mayan Vision Quest: Mystical Initiation in Mesoamerica*, San Francisco, 1991

MUS, PAUL, *Barabudur*, 2 vols, New York, 1978

NEUMANN, ERICH, *The Psychological Meaning of Ritual*, Quadrant 9 (1976)

NEUSNER, JACOB, 'Map Without Territory: Mishnah's System of Sacrifice and Sanctuary', *History of Religions 19* (1979), pp. 103–27

NIBLEY, HUGH, *The Message of the Joseph Smith Papyri, an Egyptian Endowment*, Salt Lake City, 1975

———, *Temple and Cosmos*, ed. Don E. Norton (The Collected Works of Hugh Nibley, vol. 12), Salt Lake City, 1992

OLSCHAK, BLANCHE CHRISTINE, in collaboration with GESHE THUPTEN WANGYAL, *Mystic Art of Ancient Tibet*, Boston, 1987

RAPPAPORT, ROY A., 'The Obvious Aspects of Ritual', *Ecology, Meaning, and Religion*, Richmond, Calif., 1979, pp. 173–221

SAUREN, H., *Die Einweihung des Enninu*, Istanbul, 1975

SCHELE, LINDA, and DAVID FREIDEL, *A Forest of Kings: The Untold Story of the Ancient Maya*, New York, 1990

SOEKMONO, R., *Borobudur: Prayer in Stone*, London, 1990

STENCEL, ROBERT, FRED GIFFORD and ELEANOR MORON, 'Astrology and Cosmology at Angkor Wat', *Science*, 193 (July 23, 1976), pp. 281–87

TUCCI, GIUSEPPE, *The Theory and Practice of the Mandala*, trans. Alan Houghton Brodrick, New York, 1970

VARRO, MARCUS TERENTIUS, *On the Latin Language*, Cambridge, Mass., 1951

VON SIMSON, OTTO, *The Gothic Cathedral* (Bollingen Series, XLVII), Princeton, 1988 (3rd edn)

WAYMAN, ALEX, *The Buddhist Tantras: New Light on Indo-Tibetan Esotericism*, New York, 1974

ZIMMER, HEINRICH, *Artistic Form and Yoga in the Sacred Images of India*, Princeton, 1984

ACKNOWLEDGMENTS

Numbers refer to page numbers

a=above, c= centre, b=below, l=left, r=right

The objects and illustrations reproduced in this book are in the following collections: ARCHAEOLOGICAL MUSEUM, Delphi 103tr | DET ARNAMAGNAEANSKE INSTITUT, University of Copenhagen, photo Bent Mann Nielsen (AM 738) 118r | GERTRUDE BELL COLLECTION, University of Newcastle-upon-Tyne 115br | BIBLIOTHÈQUE INGUIMBERTINE, Carpentras, France (MS 412) 8 | BIBLIOTHÈQUE NATIONALE, Paris (MS Lat. 8850) 21, (MS Sup. P. 1567) 25, (MS lat. 8878) 33, (MS Ar. 2278) 109br, (MS Grec 1208) 121bl, (MS Néerl. 3) 120bl | Reproduced by courtesy of the Trustees of THE BRITISH MUSEUM, London 62, 69, 71, 76–77, 102b, 117t, 119tr | L'ECOLE DE BEAUX ARTS, Paris 65 | Courtesy WILLIAM K. EHRENFELD. Painting illustrated in *Indian Miniatures. The Ehrenfeld Collection* (1985) 81 | FREER GALLERY OF ART, Washington, D.C. 60 | GOTLANDS FORNSAL, Visby 111cr | IKONENMUSEUM, Recklinghausen 107bl | INDIAN MUSEUM, Calcutta 104b | ISRAEL MUSEUM, Jerusalem 84 | KONINKLIJK MUSEUM VOOR SCHONE KUNSTEN, Antwerp 59 | KWUZAT HELFZIBAH, Beth-alpha Synagogue, Israel 114r | Louvre, Paris 79, 108br, 109cl | All rights reserved THE METROPOLITAN MUSEUM OF ART, New York, Helen H. Mertens Gift Fund 1973 (1973.11.3), 93l | Musée GUIMET, Paris 111b | Museo Nationale, Naples 63 | MUSEO NACIONAL DE ANTROPOLOGIA, Mexico D.F. 6, 102tr | NATIONAL ARCHEOLOGICAL MUSEUM, Athens 123bl | Reproduced by courtesy of the Trustees, THE NATIONAL GALLERY, London 7 | NATIONAL MUSEUM OF FINLAND, Helsinki 107tr | NATIONAL MUSEUM OF INDIA, New Delhi 103bl | Collection of the NEWARK MUSEUM, Newark. Purchase 1920 Albert L. Shelton Collection. Photo John Bigelow Taylor, 1991, N.Y.C. 31 | NEW YORK PUBLIC LIBRARY, Oriental Division 12, 38, 102b, 108bl, 121tr, 122t, 123tl | NEW YORK PUBLIC LIBRARY, Spencer Collection (MS No. 30) 107tl | ÖSTERREICHISCHE NATIONALBIBLIOTHEK, Vienna (*Codex Vindobensis Mexicanus I*) 119br | S. PETRONIO, Bologna 29 | SMITHSONIAN INSTITUTION, Washington, D.C. 107cr | STAATLICHE MUSEEN, Berlin 120br | STAATSGALERIE, Stuttgart 101tl | TOPKAPI SARAYI MÜZESI KÜTÜPHANESI, Istanbul (Hazine 2154, 107) 106t | By courtesy of the Board of Trustees of the VICTORIA AND ALBERT MUSEUM, London 20, 122b.

Sources of illustrations: Photo AKG-IMAGES/JEAN LOUIS NOU 57 | Photo ANTIKVARISK TOPOGRAFISKA ARKIVET, Stockholm (H. Faith-Ell) 125t | EL ARABY MAGAZINE 66 | ARCHIVE FOR RESEARCH IN ARCHETYPAL SYMBOLISM 123bl | Photo ARTHAUD 26, 104t, 121br | Photo ARTHUAD/M. AUDRAIN 105bl | After F. BALTZER, *Die Architektur der Kultbauten Japan* (1907) 63 | H. BARADÈRE, *Trois Expeditions du Capitaine Dupaix* (1834) 97 | J. F. CHAMPOLLION, *Monuments de l'Egypte et de la Nubie* (1835–45) 12 | Photo CRAIG CHIASSON/ISTOCKPHOTO. COM 83 | E. CHASSINAT, *Le Temple d'Edlou*, vol. 12 (1934) 38, 108l | Photo COMPANIA MEXICANA AEROFOTO, S.A. 109bl | A. B. COOK, *Zeus*, vol. 11 (1925) 103br | Photo ROY C. CRAVEN 100bl | DAILY TRAVEL PHOTOS/ www. ISTOCKPHOTO.COM 15 | T. and W. DANIELL, *Antiquities of India, 1799–1808* 105tr, 118c, 118l | *Description de l'Egypte* (1798) 122t | Photo DIRECTORATE GENERAL, Department of Antiquities, Iraq 16 | Photo RICHARD DORMER 23 | Photo JEREMY EDWARDS/WWW.ISTOCKPHOTO.COM 42 | Photo DR CAROLYN ELLIOTT 116r | J. GAILHABAUD, *L'Architecture du Vme au XVIIme Siècle* (1858) 84 | Photo GEORG GERSTER/JOHN HILLELSON AGENCY 51 | Photo HEIDI GRASSLEY © Thames & Hudson Ltd, London 37, 86, 90, 91, 92 | Photo STEVEN GUSTAFSON/ISTOCKPHOTO.COM 35 | Photo NICHOLAS HELLMUTH 44 | HIRMER FOTOARCHIV, Munich 101br, 110r, 123bl | Photo C. GREG HURSLEY/HURSLEY/LARK/HURSLEY 119bl | Photo INSTITUT GÉOGRAPHIQUE NATIONAL, Paris 125b | Photo INSTITUTO NACIONAL DE ANTROPOLOGIA E HISTORIA, Mexico D.F., 102tr | Photo IRISH TOURIST BOARD 116l | G. JEQUIER, *l'Architecture et la Décoration dans l'Ancienne Egypte* (1920) 121tr | Photo RUSSELL JOHNSON 54 | Photo A. F. KERSTING 114l | Photo JAMES HARRISON/ISTOCKPHOTO.COM 73 | B. LAMY, *De Tabernaculo Foederis* (Paris, 1720) 115bl | Photo RICHARD LANNOY 22 | Photo LIU LIZHONG 61 | G. LOUD and C. B. ALTMAN, *Khorsabad. The Citadel and Town* (1938) 123tl | Photo JOHN LUNDQUIST 30, 53, 103tl, 112t, 113, 117b, 121tl | Photo SALLY NICOLLS 41 | J. NIEUHOF, *An Embassy ... to China* (1669) 19 | T. PATCH and F. GREGORI, *Libro della Seconda e Terza Porta di bronzo della Chiesa di Giovanni Battista di Firenze* (1774) 107br | Photo SEMITOUR PERIGORD 67 | Photo JOSEPHINE POWELL 105tl, 119tl | © RMN Paris 108r, 109cl | D. ROBERTS, *Egypt and Nubia*, 87 | Photo: ROBERT D. RUBIK NYC 12, 38, 102b, 108l, 121tr, 122t, 123tl | Photo ALBERT SHOUCAIR 89 | Photo SMPK, ANTIKENMUSEUM, Berlin 93r | Photo KIRILL TRIFONOV/ISTOCKPHOTO.COM 112b | Photo JEAN VERTUT 75, 109tl | Photo STEVEN VIDLER/EURASIA PRESS/CORBIS 85 | Copyright A. C. WESTERN 47 | Photo RICHARD H. WILKINSON 70 | L. WOOLLEY, *Ur Excavations. The Ziggurat and its Surroundings* (1939) 100tl.

INDEX

Page numbers in *italic* refer to illustrations.